Basics of California Law
for LMFTs, LPCCs, and LCSWs
Third edition (2015)

Benjamin E. Caldwell, PsyD

Basics of California Law for LMFTs, LPCCs, and LCSWs
Third edition (2015)

ISBN 978-0-9888759-5-1

This edition: January 2015
Previous editions:
      First edition: January 2013
          Minor revision, noted as 2013.1 edition: March 2013
      Second edition: January 2014

Benjamin E. Caldwell, PsyD
6222 Wilshire Blvd, Suite 200
Los Angeles CA 90048

www.bencaldwell.com
ben@bencaldwell.com

Ordering Information:

Special discounts are available on bulk purchases by educators, corporations, associations, and others. For details, contact the publisher at the above listed address.

U.S. trade bookstores and wholesalers: Please contact Benjamin E. Caldwell, 323-246-8823, or email ben@bencaldwell.com.

*To those therapists
past, present, and future
working to make the rules work better*

▶ Acknowledgments

Translating California law to something approaching English is no easy task, especially for someone like me who is a practicing clinician and not a lawyer. My humblest and most sincere thanks go to all of those who have assisted with this project in ways big and small.

I am indebted to my colleagues at Alliant International University, Caldwell-Clark, AAMFT, AAMFT-California Division, Noteware Government Relations, the California Board of Behavioral Sciences, and many others for their suggestions, support, and guidance as I have learned about the laws of California and the process of changing them. I am particularly indebted to Angela Kahn for her help, advice, and review of early drafts of this edition, and to Aimee Clark, Diane Gehart, Olivia Loewy, and Scott Woolley – friends and brilliant therapists all – for their support along the way.

My thanks as well to Chris Caldwell, editor extraordinaire, talented fisherman, and wonderful father, for making the 2013.1 edition (and by extension those that have followed) so darned readable. Would that I could write like that man does.

My thanks to the many students and faculty who have used and offered comments on earlier editions of this book, at Alliant, California State University Northridge, the Wright Institute, and many other universities around California.

Finally, my thanks to everyone else who has offered feedback and suggestions based on real-world use of this book. I am sure I missed naming some important people here, and for that I can only offer my apologies. I am profoundly grateful to each of you.

▶ About this guide / Disclaimers

This guide is focused on state law as of January 2015 unless otherwise noted; laws change quickly, and it is the responsibility of the therapist to stay current. In addition, **this guide is a summary**; it is **not meant to cover every situation a therapist may encounter related to the topics discussed here. The author assumes no liability for errors, omissions, or changes in law. Additional state and federal laws beyond those mentioned here may govern your work based on your clientele and work setting.**

This guide is for informational purposes only, and reflects a clinician's plain-language reading of the law. No part of it may be construed as legal advice. This text is NOT a substitute for consultation with a qualified attorney. I am an educator and a practicing Marriage and Family Therapist, and not an attorney. If you are in need of legal advice, I strongly encourage you to make use of the legal resources available to you through your professional association and your professional liability insurance carrier.

Links to online resources are presented here for reference purposes only. Any link to an outside resource should not be viewed as an endorsement of that resource (or as the resource endorsing this book). While every effort has been made to ensure that the links here were functional and accurate as of the time of writing, information and links on the Internet change frequently. It cannot be guaranteed that the links presented here are current or accurate. The author assumes no responsibility for the accuracy, currency, or completeness of information on linked web sites, or for the functionality of those sites.

▶ Copyright notice

Contents

Detailed Contents

Introduction (or Why You Need This Book) 15

1. Scope of Practice   23

3. Unprofessional Conduct

4. Informed Consent   115

5. Confidentiality, Privilege, and Exceptions

7. Working with Elders and Dependent Adults

8. Advertising   189

9. Technology

10. Advocating for Changes in Law, Regulation, or Policy

Appendices

Introduction
(or Why You Need This Book)

There are three sets of rules that govern mental health work: **Laws**, **ethics**, and the **standard of care.** Laws trump everything else; if there is a direct conflict between your professional code of ethics and the law, the law generally wins (although you should follow the law with the strongest possible adherence to the ethics code).[1] If one simply sets a higher standard than another, then following that higher standard should mean you are behaving in both a legal and ethical manner.

Laws are developed by legislators and regulators. The laws that govern a profession generally focus on what you *must* or *must not* do within your professional role. They operate from a basis of public protection, ensuring that there is legal recourse for a client who is severely mistreated by someone entrusted to protect them. That can be important to remember as you encounter laws here that may at first seem strange or unnecessary: The laws governing mental health work are not developed *for* the professionals. They are developed to protect the public *from* professionals who might otherwise seek to take advantage of their professional status and clients' vulnerability.

Codes of ethics are developed by professional associations to help define their work, and to protect both the public and the professionals themselves. The public is protected because they can trust that a mental health professional is following a set of agreed-upon rules for their care. The professionals benefit by virtue of less government regulation (lawmakers are much more reluctant to add regulations to a profession when the profession seems to be adequately governing itself). Sound ethics codes also help shield

---

[1] AAMFT Code of Ethics preamble; ACA Code of Ethics subprinciple I.1.c; NASW Code of Ethics preamble

professionals against malpractice lawsuits, since professionals can use them to demonstrate they have followed standard rules of the profession.

Codes of ethics vary in their design, with some written more narrowly to make enforcement easier, and others written with more aspirational language to help guide professionals in what ideal behavior looks like. In the mental health professions, ethical codes often seek to achieve both enforceability and guidance for more ideal behavior. When the American Association for Marriage and Family Therapy (AAMFT) updated its Code of Ethics for 2015,[2] they added aspirational elements for the first time. The National Association of Social Workers (NASW) Code of Ethics[3] is a good example of a code that includes significant guidance not just on what social workers are required to do or not do, but also on the kinds of behavior they strive for.

Regardless of an ethics code's design, there will invariably be times when elements of the code fail to offer clear guidance to a therapist wondering how to handle a particular situation, and times when different parts of the code appear to conflict. One recent and controversial example has been the problem of religious therapists refusing to treat gay and lesbian clients. While such refusals would appear to violate the anti-discrimination clauses of each profession's code of ethics, the therapists involved would argue that if they were forced to provide treatment to a population their religious beliefs preclude them from supporting, they would be violating the ethics clauses demanding competent treatment.

In situations where there is no clear legal or ethical guidance, therapists are expected to follow the *standard of care* for their field. Essentially, the standard of care is whatever practices most other people in the profession are following in a particular situation. This is why it is so important, and so helpful, to consult with colleagues and supervisors when you are unsure how to best handle a situation. Gathering ideas from those you trust in the field can help you to know whether a standard of care exists for your specific situation, and if so, how to best follow it.

---

[2] AAMFT Code of Ethics
[3] NASW Code of Ethics

Your best sources of information when seeking a specific, applicable standard of care for your situation are writings in the field, and your supervisors and colleagues. As should be obvious, the best sources of information when it comes to ethical guidelines are the codes of ethics themselves (their web addresses appear in the appendices at the end of this book). There are also a number of great texts offering general discussion of legal and ethical issues in the mental health professions. But the mental health professions are regulated at the state level. Where can you go to learn about the *California* laws that govern Licensed Marriage and Family Therapists (LMFTs), Licensed Professional Clinical Counselors (LPCCs), and Licensed Clinical Social Workers (LCSWs)?

I wrote this book to be the answer to that question.

For the actual language of the law, you can download the free compilation put together every year by the Board of Behavioral Sciences (BBS), our licensing board.[4] However, there is nothing to translate that legal language to plain English, and it can often be difficult to find the specific information you are looking for.

This book aims to make that easier. While it is, by design, a summary – state law offers many more specific rules than could be covered here – it seeks to address key elements you need to know as a practitioner.

How to use this book

Depending on where you are in your career, you may have purchased this text as a class requirement, as part of preparing for your license exams, or as a general reference. I hope that it works well as any of those. I have tried to make each chapter as independent as possible, so that if what you really need is information about child abuse reporting, as one example, you can simply jump ahead to that chapter.

You will notice more than 400 footnotes in this text, most of which include specific references to sections of law or other relevant information. Please make use of them! Doing so will help you to learn

---

[4] Board of Behavioral Sciences (2014). *Statutes and Regulations Relating to the Practice of Professional Clinical Counseling, Marriage and Family Therapy, Educational Psychology, and Clinical Social Work.* Sacramento, CA: BBS.

about the language and structure of the law itself. They also can help clarify any elements of this text you are having struggles with.

It is worth repeating here the disclaimer that appears before the Table of Contents. **While I hope this book is a valuable reference, it is NOT a substitute for legal advice from a qualified attorney.** This book does not cover every situation you will encounter, nor does it include every state law impacting mental health work. Laws and regulations can change quickly, so I can't be held responsible for errors or omissions here. I am a practicing LMFT who teaches law and ethics for a university, and I am **not** an attorney. If you are in need of legal advice, you can likely get it at no charge from your professional association or your professional liability insurance carrier.

Links

Internet addresses referenced in this text are to official sources whenever possible. Of course, information online changes quickly, so I cannot assume any responsibility for the accuracy or functioning of any of the sites linked here. But I hope you will find the links to be useful when you want more in-depth knowledge or direct legal language on the issues covered here.

Some notes on terminology

Throughout this guide, I use the following acronyms:

BBS - The California Board of Behavioral Sciences, which is the state licensing board for Professional Clinical Counselors, Clinical Social Workers, and Marriage and Family Therapists. The BBS also licenses Educational Psychologists (LEPs), however, LEPs are not a focus of this text.
LCSW – Licensed Clinical Social Worker.
LPCC – Licensed Professional Clinical Counselor.
LMFT – Licensed Marriage and Family Therapist.

I also use the following terms to refer to stages of the licensing ladder. These terms apply to all three professions (marriage and family therapy, clinical social work, and professional clinical counseling):

Licensee – Those who are fully and actively licensed by the Board of Behavioral Sciences (LMFTs, LCSWs, and LPCCs). If you are not yet fully licensed, you are not a licensee.

Registrant – MFT and PCC interns, and CSW associates. Such individuals have completed their master's degrees and are registered with the BBS but are not licensed.

Trainee – Those who are completing required experience as part of their graduate degree program. These individuals are not licensed or registered with the BBS, but their work is still governed by California law and regulation.

What's new in the third edition

This update includes a wide variety of changes. Some, of course, are simply designed to keep the book current with California law. Others are responses to trends in the mental health professions. In this edition, new material has been incorporated into almost every chapter.

For readers familiar with earlier editions of this book, the most obvious changes are in its formatting. In addition to the change in size, previous section divisions have been removed, and tables are all now numbered for easier reference (including a new list of tables in the Appendices).

The content changes, however, are much more significant. Throughout the book, references to professional ethical codes for counselors and family therapists have been updated to be consistent with the new codes from ACA (2014) and AAMFT (2015). In Chapter 1, there is new discussion on the ethics of seeing clients across state lines by phone or Internet. In Chapter 2, I have included discussion of a legislative proposal that would dramatically restructure how hours of experience are categorized for licensure for MFTs and PCCs. In Chapter 3, there are several additions: there is a new legal standard in California for the retention of clinical records, the BBS is adopting new disciplinary standards for substance-related violations, and I've added some discussion of how well-meaning therapists using social media can violate the unprofessional conduct statutes by getting too specific about what was on their licensing exams. Chapter 4 now includes discussion of social media in informed consent, and addresses the importance of clarifying for clients who exactly qualifies as "the client." Chapter 5 also covers the state's new standards for retaining records.

In Chapter 6, there is discussion of a problematic new law intended to stop digital distribution of child pornography. This chapter also now includes information on California's first-in-the-nation ban on so-called "reparative therapy," or therapeutic attempts to change a minor's sexual orientation. Chapter 7 is the only chapter in the book to not see substantive changes in this edition, though it (like every chapter) has had some small changes to clean up typos and improve readability. Chapters 8 and 9 are the most changed. In Chapter 8, there is new discussion of networking groups, doctoral students using the initials "ABD" ("All But Dissertation"), and ethical requirements for therapist web sites and social media presences. I've also made note that the BBS has new cite-and-fine authority over non-compliant advertising. I've updated information on acceptable abbreviations for PCC interns, and on the use of testimonials for all three professions covered in this book. In Chapter 9, I've added information on organizations that specialize in telehealth issues for health care providers, and updated the ethical requirements for therapists' use of technology (Table 9.1). Finally, in Chapter 10, I've added information on how California's reparative therapy ban came into being.

Those are just the high points. Throughout the book there are also dozens of changes and additions to keep the information here current and, hopefully, easy to read.

Feedback

As you read above, this is the third edition of this book. Each time it has been revised, some of the changes have been to keep it current with state law, and other changes have been to make it more readable, often in response to reader suggestions. Your feedback can help make future editions of this book even better! I would love to hear your comments and suggestions. You can send them to me by email at ben@bencaldwell.com. As I said, I'm not a lawyer, so please do not send any questions requesting legal advice; those are better directed to an attorney.

Let's get started!

anxiety. The different mental health professions will likely start from very different places as they seek to answer the question, "Why is Diego struggling with anxiety?"

Psychology

Although this text does not focus on Psychologists, understanding their perspective can be helpful. **A traditional Psychologist would examine Diego's inner world to find the root of his dysfunction.** Whether looking to his childhood (as a Freudian would) or looking to his present (as a behaviorist would), the focus will be on Diego as an individual. Furthermore, traditional psychology would focus on pathology – rooting out what is wrong with Diego individually.[5]

Professional Clinical Counseling

The professional clinical counseling field emerged from school and career counseling. While they focus today on mental health, **LPCCs are likely to see Diego's struggle as an individual, developmental issue.** They will examine his psychological and social development and his current functioning, and treatment will focus on helping Diego improve overall development and wellness (including treatment of mental illness).

Clinical Social Work

Clinical social workers place their focus on connecting people with the resources they need to function well. Those resources may be internal (such as personal skills and strengths, some of which Diego may not be utilizing to their potential) or external (such as community resources and support groups). Traditionally speaking, **LCSWs are likely to see Diego's struggle as a resource issue,** and will work with Diego to gather the internal and external resources needed for him to control and ultimately overcome his anxiety.

---

[5] Yes, this is an oversimplification, and today's field of Psychology is much more expansive. We'll get there. Stay with me.

Marriage and Family Therapy

LMFTs look at behavior in its social and relational context. Perhaps Diego's anxiety has emerged as a result of tension in his work or in his relationships. Perhaps his anxiety is even adaptive when considered in its context – for example, if he receives more support from his boss or from his partner when showing outward signs of anxiety. Ultimately, LMFTs believe that no behavior exists in a social vacuum, and will work with Diego – as well as other family members and other important people in Diego's life, if appropriate – in an effort to make the anxiety no longer necessary.

Areas of overlap

As you can see, **none of these philosophies is any better or worse than the others. They're just different.** That matters a great deal as new professionals are being trained and socialized into their respective professions. Of course, the perspectives above are purist ones, and even looking at things from that purist perspective, there is significant overlap between these philosophies for dealing with many problems. When handling adjustment issues with children, for example, LMFTs and LPCCs may work very similarly.

Each of these fields has also been influenced by the others. Using Psychologists as an example, there are now Community Psychologists (who share a great deal in common with LCSWs in their approach), Family Psychologists (who share a great deal in common with LMFTs), and Counseling Psychologists (who share a great deal in common with LPCCs). The professions all benefit from this cross-pollination, which helps us communicate effectively with one another and assess clients more thoroughly. But, using LMFTs as an example, one only needs examine the core competencies for LMFTs[6] to see where the overlap ends; even just reading through the list of skills all LMFTs are expected to be able to do, they can be broken down roughly equally into three categories:

---

[6] American Association for Marriage and Family Therapy (2004). *Marriage and family therapy core competencies.* Alexandria, VA: AAMFT.

1. Tasks that all mental health professionals should be able to do, and that all would do about the same way (for example, suicide assessment).
2. Tasks that all mental health professionals should be able to do, but LMFTs would do from a different conceptual framework.
3. Tasks that LMFTs should be able to do that other mental health professionals would not necessarily be expected to do.

Of course, LMFTs are not superior to the other professions, nor do they have greater job functions. I'm just using LMFTs as an example. A list of core competencies for LCSWs or for LPCCs could surely be broken down into similar proportions. The point is, while we all do many of the same things in assessing, diagnosing, and treating mental illness, it is quite a disservice to the professions to suggest we are all the same.

▶ Defining "scope of practice"

A profession's scope of practice outlines the activities one can legally do as part of that profession. It helps define the boundaries of a profession, and the differences between one profession and another. An LCSW is allowed to practice therapy, but not brain surgery, because of the different scopes of practice between LCSWs and physicians.

All of the master's-level mental health professions discussed here are able to perform psychotherapy within their scope of practice. (Using the terms "psychotherapy" and "psychotherapist" in advertising does come with specific additional requirements. See Chapter 8.)

Scope of practice vs. scope of competence

Of course, you will never be an expert in *everything* that can be done under your license. In order to engage in any activity as a professional, in addition to that activity being within your profession's legal scope of practice, that activity also must belong to your personal scope of competence. Your scope of competence consists of those activities that you have appropriate education, training, and experience to do on your own.

For you visual learners, here's the difference in table form:

Table 1.1: Scope of practice vs. scope of competence

	Scope of Practice	Scope of Competence
Applies to:	**Everyone in your profession equally**	**You specifically**
Defined by:	**State law**	**Your education, training, and experience**
Can you expand yours?	**No** (unless you get additional licenses)	**Yes**, through additional education, training, and experience

▶ Marriage and family therapy scope of practice

Normally in this text, I present a clinician's understanding of state law, and offer references to the actual letter of the law. When dealing with scope of practice, it is often helpful to review the actual letter of the law, so I've copied it below – with some notes to help you understand its meaning.

LMFT Scope of Practice in CA law[7]

For the purposes of this chapter, the practice of marriage and family therapy shall mean that service performed with individuals, couples, or groups wherein interpersonal relationships are examined for the purpose of achieving more adequate, satisfying, and productive marriage and family adjustments. This practice includes relationship and pre-marriage counseling.

(Continued on the next page)

A clinician's translation

→ LMFTs do not just work with couples and families; they work with individuals and groups as well.

→ This nicely lays out the relational philosophy of LMFTs: They examine people in their relational context, and work to make that relational context more satisfying.

[7] California Business and Professions Code section 4980.02

LMFT Scope of Practice in CA law[8]

(continued)

The application of marriage and family therapy principles and methods includes, but is not limited to, the use of applied psychotherapeutic techniques, to enable individuals to mature and grow within marriage and the family, the provision of explanations and interpretations of the psychosexual and psychosocial aspects of relationships, and the use, application, and integration of the coursework and training required by Sections 4980.36, 4980.37, and 4980.41.

A clinician's translation

This phrase establishes LMFTs as psychotherapists, and was key to the determination that LMFTs can legally use psychological tests. Testing is an "applied psychotherapeutic technique."

While the words "assess," "diagnose," and "treat" are not anywhere in the LMFT scope of practice language, they are required to be trained in these skills – and this passage in the LMFT scope of practice means they are allowed to use those skills to assess, diagnose, and treat in practice.

[8] California Business and Professions Code section 4980.02

Restriction on psychological testing

LMFTs are restricted in their ability to perform psychological tests. **Contrary to a common misunderstanding among mental health professionals, LMFTs in California <u>are</u> allowed to do psychological testing. They simply must meet two conditions:**

- The LMFT must have appropriate training in the instrument used.
- Testing must be case-specific and within a therapeutic context. That is, LMFTs can do psychological testing only in the context of an ongoing therapy relationship.[9]

These conditions are specified in a 1984 California Attorney General's opinion, which has the power of law. It emerged after a long and contentious debate between Psychologists and LMFTs about whether such testing was within the LMFT scope. As we will see, Psychologists did not want to repeat this debate when LPCCs sought licensure in California, so they negotiated very specific language into the LPCC scope of practice that defines counselors' ability to perform psychological tests.

---

[9] Van de Kamp, J. K. (1984). *Do marriage, family and child counselors have the statutory authority to construct, administer, and interpret psychological tests?* California Attorney General opinion no. 83-810, June 28, 1984.

▶ Professional clinical counseling scope of practice

Professional clinical counselors are the newest mental health professionals in California. The LPCC scope of practice language came together after years of negotiations with the BBS and other mental health professions in California. As a result, it is much more detailed than the scopes of the other professions.

LPCC Scope of Practice in CA law[10]	A clinician's translation
(1) "Professional clinical counseling" means the application of counseling interventions and psychotherapeutic techniques to identify and remediate cognitive, mental, and emotional issues, including personal growth, adjustment to disability, crisis intervention, and psychosocial and environmental problems, and the use, application, and integration of the coursework and training required by Sections 4999.32 and 4999.33. *(Continued on the next page)*	This establishes LPCCs as psychotherapists. As is the case for LMFTs, the LPCC scope does not directly use the words "assess," "diagnose," or "treat" in relation to mental illness. But this language makes clear that these tasks are within the LPCC scope. LPCCs' scope includes the assessment, diagnosis, and treatment of mental disorders.

[10] California Business and Professions Code section 4999.20(a)

LPCC Scope of Practice in CA law[11]	A clinician's translation
(continued)	
(2) "Professional clinical counseling" includes conducting assessments for the purpose of establishing counseling goals and objectives to empower individuals to deal adequately with life situations, reduce stress, experience growth, change behavior, and make well-informed rational decisions.	This allows LPCCs to use psychological tests, but there are important limitations on this. See the next page.
(3) "Professional clinical counseling" is focused exclusively on the application of counseling interventions and psychotherapeutic techniques for the purposes of improving mental health, and is not intended to capture other, nonclinical forms of counseling for the purposes of licensure. For the purposes of this paragraph, "nonclinical" means nonmental health.	This language clarifies that career and other non-mental-health counselors do not need an LPCC license.

[11] California Business and Professions Code section 4999.20(a)

Restriction on working with couples and families

Because they are not required to have any training or supervised experience working with couples and families prior to licensure, **LPCCs are prohibited from assessing or treating couples and families in practice unless they have completed all of the following:**

- **6 semester units or 9 quarter units of coursework** in couple and family therapy, **or a named specialization in couple and family therapy** on their degree
- **500 hours supervised experience** with couples, families, and children
- **6 hours of continuing education on couple and family work** in each renewal cycle[12]

Of course, PCC interns and trainees (and, for that matter, licensees) who are under supervision and working toward the completion of these requirements are able to see couples and families. Indeed, many of those who complete these requirements (excepting CE, which is after licensure) do so within their regular degree program and supervised experience.

Because working with children necessarily involves working with their families (see Chapter 6, Working with Minors), LPCCs wishing to work with children would be wise to complete these additional requirements.

Restriction on psychological testing

Professional clinical counselors are able to use psychological tests and measures. However, **LPCCs are explicitly prohibited from using any of the following testing procedures:**[13]

---

[12] California Business & Professions Code section 4999.20(a)(3)
[13] California Business & Professions Code section 4999.20(c)

- Projective tests of personality (such as the Rorschach)
- Individually administered intelligence tests
- Neuropsychological testing
- Utilization of a battery of three or more tests to assess psychosis, dementia, amnesia, cognitive impairment, or criminal behavior

"Assessment" as it relates to tests and measures for LPCCs is also specifically defined as an activity done "as part of the counseling process."[14] This would appear to mean that, similar to LMFTs, LPCCs cannot conduct psychological evaluations with people who are not engaged in an ongoing therapy process with the LPCC.

Additional definitions

The LPCC scope language includes two other important definitions. First, it clarifies that "professional counseling does not include the provision of clinical social work services."[15] That is simply a recognition (one of several in the LPCC licensing act) that LPCCs and LCSWs practice distinct professions.

Second, the bill includes a definition of "counseling interventions and psychotherapeutic techniques" that reinforces the philosophical distinctiveness of the LPCC profession. It notes that while LPCCs work in a variety of ways, using many different theories and approaches, all LPCCs' interventions "include principles of development, wellness, and maladjustment."[16] Note how this ties into the discussion earlier in this chapter about the underlying LPCC philosophy and how it relates to the other masters-level mental health professions.

---

[14] California Business & Professions Code section 4999.20(c)
[15] California Business & Professions Code section 4999.20(a)(4)
[16] California Business & Professions Code section 4999.20(b)

▶ Clinical social work scope of practice

The clinical social work scope of practice skillfully integrates LCSWs' roles as psychotherapists with the values traditionally underlying social work in all its forms. Notice the inclusion of terms like "resources," "human capabilities," and "potential."

LCSW Scope of Practice in CA law[17]	A clinician's translation
The practice of clinical social work is defined as a service in which a special knowledge of social resources, human capabilities, and the part that unconscious motivation plays in determining behavior, is directed at helping people to achieve more adequate, satisfying, and productive social adjustments. The application of social work principles and methods includes, but is not restricted to, counseling and using applied psychotherapy of a nonmedical nature with individuals, families, or groups; providing information and referral services;	This is a reference to how social workers are trained. The term "special knowledge" makes clear that this training is distinct from that given to other professionals.

This establishes LCSWs as psychotherapists. Psychotherapy, for the purposes of the LCSW scope, is defined in the next paragraph (see next page). |

(Continued on the next page)

[17] California Business and Professions Code section 4996.9

LCSW Scope of Practice in CA law[18]

A clinician's translation

(continued)

providing or arranging for
the provision of social
services; explaining or
interpreting the psychosocial
aspects in the situations of
individuals, families, or
groups; helping communities
to organize, to provide, or
to improve social or health
services; doing research
related to social work; and
the use, application, and
integration of the coursework
and experience required by
sections 4996.2 and 4996.23.

Psychotherapy, within the
meaning of this chapter, is
the use of psychosocial
methods within a professional
relationship, to assist the
person or persons to achieve
a better psychosocial
adaptation, to acquire
greater human realization of
psychosocial potential and
adaptation, to modify
internal and external
conditions which affect
individuals, groups, or
communities in respect to
behavior, emotions, and
thinking, in respect to their
intrapersonal and
interpersonal processes.

This makes clear that LCSWs
are not limited to working with
individuals. They also can work
with couples, families, and groups.

This language, a parallel to the
LMFT and LPCC scopes, was
added in 2014. It clarifies, as one
example, that LCSWs can do
substance abuse treatment, as this
is required in their training under
section 4996.2.

This is the closest the LCSW
language gets to saying that
LCSWs assess, diagnose, and treat
the full range of mental and
emotional disorders. As is the case
for the other professions, the
integration of required training
(see above) makes clear that
LCSWs can perform those tasks.

[18] California Business and
Professions Code section 4996.9

4

▶ Interns, associates, and trainees

> **There are no differences in the legal scope of practice for a licensed professional compared with someone working toward licensure in that profession.** However, scope of *competence* becomes very important.

Clinical counselors and family therapists who have completed their graduate degrees and are working on their supervised hours of experience for licensure are referred to in the law as "interns," while Clinical Social Workers at the same stage are referred to as "associates." For all three professions, those who are completing a practicum experience as part of their degree program are referred to as "trainees."

Interns, associates, and trainees in each of these professions have the same scope of practice as those who are licensed; while there are some activities trainees cannot take part in (like supervision via videoconferencing), the acceptable clinical activities of licensees and prelicensees are largely the same. However, **interns, associates, and trainees must be under supervision, and trainees must be engaging in their work as part of a recognized degree program.**[19] In addition, there are a number of non-clinical restrictions on what interns, associates, and trainees can do. They cannot be paid directly by clients, and they cannot rent their own office space, as two examples.[20]

Interns, associates and trainees must also be especially mindful of their scope of competence (see earlier in this chapter for a definition of the term). While the law may allow them to do largely the same range of clinical activities as licensed practitioners, they are still subject to the limits of their training, education, and experience – and they bump up against those limits much more regularly. Indeed, when you are early in your career, the only way to get the experience needed to expand your competence is by working (under supervision) with client and problem types that are new to you.

---

[19] California Business and Professions Code section 4999.24
[20] California Business and Professions Code sections 4980.43(h) and (i), 4996.23(l), 4999.47(b)

Consider the example of an Associate Clinical Social Worker working with a teenage client who is self-injuring. There is nothing in the CSW scope of practice to prohibit the associate from doing such work. However, if the associate does not have experience in working with self-injuring clients, it is essential that they be closely supervised as they develop that experience. A good supervisor will recognize the limits of their supervisees' competence and work closely with them, providing guidance, consultation, support, and resources, to aid in the development of that competence.

▶ Licensure stops at the state line

> **California therapists typically cannot provide services to people in other states.** Some states are starting to consider making exceptions, however, and one state has done so.

Your license or registration is issued by the state of California, and only allows you to practice within the state of California. Providing services by phone or Internet to a client who is in another state at the time of the service could be considered practicing in that other state without a license. California has prosecuted a Colorado psychiatrist who prescribed medication to a California teenager through an online pharmacy, arguing successfully that the psychiatrist was practicing in California without a license.[21] **Your scope of practice only applies in the state where you are licensed.**

For MFTs, this is reinforced in ethical code language. The California Association of Marriage and Family Therapists (CAMFT) includes this in their Code of Ethics:

> 3.11 Electronic services. Marriage and family therapists provide services by Internet or other electronic media to patients located only in jurisdictions where the therapist may lawfully provide such services.[22]

The key word there is "located." As in, the physical place where the client's body is at the time of service. You could not argue that doing therapy across state lines is acceptable because the client is a California *resident* who is on vacation or away for work; if the client is outside of the state of California, you are subject to the licensing rules of the state they are physically in at the time of service.

While the other professional codes of ethics are arguably less clear on this issue, it ultimately is a legal concern as well as an ethical one. Again, your scope of practice is set by state law, and only applies in the state where you are licensed.

---

[21] Local television news coverage: www.youtube.com/watch?v=aftPEFSHExQ
[22] CAMFT Code of Ethics, subprinciple 3.11

One exception inside the US, and many outside

Recognizing the growing mobility of Americans and the growing capacity of technology to serve as a vehicle for the delivery of health care services, a number of states have crafted laws and regulations about distance counseling. Most of these states have specifically noted that when the client is in their state, the therapy is considered to have occurred in that state, regardless of where the therapist is located. This simply reinforces that your licensure stops at the state line.

One state, Arizona, has taken a different stance. Arizona has incorporated into its rules a brief window for therapists properly qualified in other states to provide distance services to clients in Arizona under specific conditions, including that the therapist not provide services to clients in Arizona for more than 90 days of any calendar year, and that they inform the client that the services are time-limited and the therapist is not licensed in Arizona. [23]

Several other states have said they are in the process of crafting or are planning to craft rules for distance services. For now, it seems unlikely that many licensing boards would allow practitioners not licensed in their state to practice there, even for brief periods. State laws exist to protect those inside the state, and licensing boards are proceeding with caution given the likelihood that a therapist seeing a client in a different state will not be familiar with that state's rules for child abuse reporting, crisis intervention, and other important issues. In any case, the onus is on the therapist to determine whether practicing by phone or Internet with a client in another state is allowed, and to not provide that service if it is not allowed.

This calculus becomes more complicated when a client is outside of the country. Since many other countries do not have formal licensure for mental health professions (and among those that do, many only license Psychologists), you could argue that you *do* have the required qualifications to practice in a country where there are no required qualifications for your profession.

---

[23] Materials for the July 2012 meeting of the BBS Policy and Advocacy Committee meeting (see page 53 of the PDF)

Weighing the risks of seeing clients in transition

In spite of the risks involved, some therapists do continue to meet with their clients via phone or other technology while the client is out of state. The argument these therapists often make is one of *continuity of care* -- leaving a client without familiar and accessible mental health resources while they are travelling out of state for work or vacation, or as they get settled into the state to which they have permanently moved, could be seen as client abandonment. So therapists sometimes will choose to keep seeing such clients, at least on a limited-term basis.

How much risk is involved in doing this depends at least in part on the nature of the services the therapist is providing. If a therapist is merely checking in on the progress of a client who has moved, and ensuring the client is getting connected with a therapist licensed in the client's new home state, that seems likely to be a low-risk proposition. Similarly, a therapist who checks in on a client vacationing out of state in order to make sure the client is maintaining medication compliance and not experiencing any worsening of symptoms is probably not taking a significant risk by doing so. When a therapist is *providing therapy* to out-of-state clients, the risk to the therapist is higher. This risk seems particularly high if the client has moved permanently and the therapist is making no effort to transition the client to resources closer to their new home.

We are an increasingly mobile society, and as the use of technology in the delivery of psychotherapy services becomes more common, the demand for licensure to operate on a national level (rather than state by state) is likely to continue to grow.[24] Until a truly portable license can be achieved, though, the safest course of action appears to be to only see clients physically located in those places where you are authorized to provide services.

---

[24] I've argued in favor of national licensure for precisely this reason on my blog: www.psychotherapynotes.com/uncategorized/its-time-for-national-licensure-laws-in-mental-health/

▶ Life coaches, consultants, and other unlicensed professions

> **Anyone can use the title of "life coach" or "consultant."** Performing psychotherapy requires a license, but unlicensed professions argue that what they do isn't psychotherapy.

The terms "life coach," "consultant," and the like do not have title protection in California law. So anyone – regardless of training or experience – can advertise themselves under these titles. That's right: Your 18-year-old nephew could set up an office and call himself a life coach if he wanted to.

Because these professions are not licensed or otherwise defined under California law, they do not have a legal scope of practice defining what they can do. Members of these unlicensed professions run the full gamut, from those who have had years of high-quality training to those who have had no training whatsoever. Those who are responsible professionals will recognize the limits of their knowledge and experience, and make referrals to licensed mental health professionals when appropriate. However, many lack the training to even know when the behavior a client is displaying suggests a possible mental health disorder.

Some licensed mental health professionals choose to use the term "life coach" in addition to their license title when advertising. The official title is required – see Chapter 8, Advertising – but is sometimes de-emphasized, in hopes that this will bring in prospective clients who are interested in receiving help with important life decisions but are unwilling to come to "therapy" if it is called that. There is nothing stopping therapists from doing this. However, unlicensed professions (and the titles and terminology associated with them) are sometimes looked down upon by licensed mental health professionals who would rather fight the stigma associated with psychotherapy than try to market their way around it. So you might risk losing a bit of respect among your peers when pursuing that marketing gain. For some therapists, the trade-off is worth it.

2

Licensing Requirements

California's requirements for obtaining licensure in the masters-level mental health professions are unusually specific relative to the rest of the country. With the exception of Licensed Clinical Social Workers, for whom the BBS largely defers to national standards, the state sets specific curriculum requirements beyond the minimums required for graduate program accreditation. For LMFTs and LCSWs, the state also uses state exams rather than the national exams generally used elsewhere.

▶ General requirements

Licensure as a mental health professional typically involves three major requirements: A qualifying graduate degree (education), practicing under a supervisor for a specified amount of time to build skills (experience), and the successful completion of exams related to the license (exams). This chapter will detail those requirements for each of the three professions for whom this book is designed.

While we think of these as licensed professions, not everyone performing the tasks of an LMFT, LPCC, or LCSW needs a license to do so. We will also address exceptions to licensure later in this chapter.

Requirements for all mental health professionals

It is important to bear in mind that completion of the requirements for licensure only makes you *eligible* for a state license; it does not *obligate* the state to give it to you. The BBS can refuse to grant a license application for a number of reasons other than failure to complete requirements. For example, the BBS may choose not to grant licenses to individuals who have prior criminal convictions that it views as related to the functions of a clinician. All license and registration applicants must undergo a background check as part of the application process.[25]

Fees

And of course, there are the fees. Any application for a license, registration, or exam eligibility will have a fee attached to it. These fees are not designed to be profitable for the state, but rather to provide sufficient funding for the BBS to run. That is correct: your licensing board is fully supported by the fees paid by licensees and registrants. They do not use any general tax funds.

---

[25] California Code of Regulations section 480

License renewals

Licenses issued by the BBS for LMFTs, LPCCs, and LCSWs are valid for two years. To renew the license, you must complete 36 hours of continuing education (just 18 hours in your initial licensure period), including six hours in law and ethics. If you are supervising, your 36 hours of CE must also include six hours on supervision. And naturally, you must pay a renewal fee.

Exemptions from licensure

While a professional license is generally required to provide the services of a Marriage and Family Therapist, Clinical Social Worker, or Professional Clinical Counselor, the law includes a number of exemptions from licensure. These allow certain individuals, or individuals working in specific settings, to do so without being licensed by the state. The exemptions from licensure include:

Individuals working toward licensure

Of course, trainees and registrants who are under supervision and working toward a license do not need to hold that license. Such a restriction would mean that no one could ever get the experience they need to become eligible for licensing exams! They are still bound to all of the requirements of the law for responsible practice, however, and their supervisors must be appropriately qualified.

Clergy

The laws for LMFTs, LCSWs, and LPCCs specifically indicate that they do not apply to religious leaders performing services as part of their religious duties.[26] Any priest, rabbi, minister, or other religious leader may offer counseling services to the religious organization's members without a state license.

---

[26] California Business and Professions Code sections 4980.01(b), 4996.13(f), and 4999.22(c)

Other professionals

While there are meaningful differences between the BBS-governed mental health professions (see Chapter 1, Scope of Practice), there are also areas of overlap. This overlap is not meant to restrict professionals from being able to do work within their own scopes of practice.

For example, what the law defines as "client-centered advocacy" for LMFTs is quite similar to the practice of social work, but an LMFT does not need to also get an LCSW license in order to do client-centered advocacy. For all the mental health professions, their ability to perform psychotherapy doesn't mean that Psychologists can't do so. Scope of practice for any one profession will typically specify that it is not meant to restrict the scope of practice of any other profession.

Employees and volunteers at exempt settings

State law also defines a number of work settings as exempt from licensure requirements. These settings include schools, nonprofit charitable organizations, and government agencies.[27] However, many settings that are officially license-exempt choose to require their workers to meet licensure or registration standards anyway, either as a function of their reimbursement process or simply to demonstrate that they are upholding high standards for clinical work.

---

[27] California Business and Professions Code sections 4980.01(c), 4996.14, and 4999.22(d)

Basics of California Law | Licensing Requirements

Licensure statuses

As I mentioned in the Introduction, when you begin your work experience during your degree program you are an unlicensed and unregistered **Trainee** in the eyes of the state. Once you complete your degree, you register as an **Intern** (MFTs and PCCs) or **Associate** (CSWs). When you complete your supervised experience and pass your licensing exams, you become **Licensed**.

These are not the only licensure statuses, however. The state also has provisions for those who want to retain their licensure but plan to stop seeing clients on either a temporary or permanent basis.

If you stop seeing clients but plan to eventually return, you can put your license on **Inactive** status. Therapists may do this for a number of reasons, including taking time off to start a family, moving temporarily out of state, or going on an extended military deployment. While your license is on Inactive status, you cannot see clients, but you also are exempted from continuing education requirements and pay a reduced license renewal fee.

If you stop seeing clients and do not plan to start again, but are interested in retaining recognition from the state, you can put your license on **Retired** status. While you can keep your license on Retired status as long as you wish, if you want to reactivate a license after more than three years on Retired status, you must reapply for licensure and retake the licensing exams.[28]

---

[28] California Business and Professions Code sections 4984.41, 4997.1, and 4999.113

▶ Marriage and Family Therapists

> **To become an LMFT, you need a qualifying graduate degree, 3,000 hours of supervised experience, and passing scores on the state's Standard Written Exam and Written Clinical Vignette Exam.** The testing process will change in 2016.

Among the three licenses discussed in this text, at first glance it would seem that Marriage and Family Therapists have the shortest path to licensure. This is because MFTs can count a great deal of experience gained as part of their graduate degree toward the 3,000 hours of experience required for licensure.

At the same time, California's requirements for MFTs are quite different from those in the rest of the country, particularly regarding education and exams. These differences can make license portability (that is, moving into a new state and obtaining the same license there) more of a challenge for LMFTs than for members of the other professions.

The BBS has proposed legislation that would significantly change the experience requirements for MFT licensure, to improve portability and eliminate some of the challenges that currently make the road to licensure much longer than it would at first appear to be.

Education

California's curriculum requirements for graduate degrees leading to LMFT licensure are the most specific in the country.[29] California requires a master's or doctoral degree of at least 60 semester units (90 quarter units), while some other states require 48 or fewer.

---

[29] California's standards for graduate education leading to LMFT licensure changed significantly for students beginning their education on or after August 1, 2012. The discussion here is based on the new, more stringent requirements. Those who began their degrees earlier than August 2012 can qualify under the old requirements as long as they complete their degrees by 2018. Some schools adopted the new requirements early, so check with your university if you are unsure which set of requirements applies to you.

In addition, while many other states include basic curriculum requirements or defer to standards set by the Commission on Accreditation for Marriage and Family Therapy Education (COAMFTE), California requires a list of specific topic areas to be covered, and includes specific content requirements within each of those topics. For this reason, if you are currently studying outside of California but are wishing to eventually license as an MFT within California, it is vital that you make sure your degree program will meet all of California's many requirements.

Graduate degree title

In order to be licensed as an MFT with a graduate degree from within California, your degree must not only meet all of the content requirements below, but also be specifically titled "marriage, family, and child counseling," "marriage and family therapy," "couple and family therapy," "psychology," "clinical psychology," "counseling psychology," or "counseling" with an emphasis in either marriage, family, and child counseling or marriage and family therapy.[30] Degrees from out of state are evaluated as to their equivalency with California's content requirements, but may not need to have one of the specific titles listed here.

Graduate degree content

Your masters or doctoral degree must include all of the following content to be a qualifying degree for MFT licensure. Note that within many of these content areas are more specific content requirements spelled out in the law.[31]

- 60 semester units (90 quarter units) in total
- 12 semester units (18 quarter units) in "theories, principles, and methods" of psychotherapy directly related to the MFT profession and family systems work

---

[30] California Business and Professions Code section 4980.36(b)
[31] California Business and Professions Code section 4980.36(d)

- 6 semester units (9 quarter units) of practicum coursework (more on that below)
- Diagnosis, assessment, and treatment of mental illness, including psychological testing and psychopharmacology
- Developmental issues across the life span
- Family relationships and related issues, including abuse assessment and reporting, parenting, marriage, divorce, blended families, end-of-life care, grief, and more
- Cultural competency and sensitivity
- Multicultural development and cross-cultural interaction, including how this impacts the therapy process
- How socioeconomic status impacts available treatment and resources
- Personal and community resilience
- Human sexuality
- Substance use disorders and co-occurring disorders
- California law and ethics

There are several additional content areas that must be included in a qualifying graduate degree, though these can be met through credit-level coursework or through extension programs (one-day workshops or similar events that do not result in course credit). Note that the language here is simply quoting the law itself, and the law does not further specify what these content areas must include:[32]

- Case management
- Systems of care for the severely mentally ill
- Public and private services and supports available for the severely mentally ill
- Community resources for persons with mental illness and for victims of abuse
- Disaster and trauma response
- Advocacy for the severely mentally ill
- Collaborative treatment

---

[32] California Business and Professions Code section 4980.36(e)

Supervised Experience

California has unusually stringent requirements for the experience MFTs gain on the way to licensure. The supervised experience requirement for MFTs includes a number of specific types of experience that carry their own minimums or maximums.

MFTs begin seeing clients during their graduate degree programs. **When a student is completing required hours of clinical experience as part of their graduate degree, they are considered to be an MFT Trainee.** The experience they are completing is called a *practicum*. **Once they graduate, the MFT-in-training applies to the BBS to become a Marriage and Family Therapist Registered Intern until they move ahead to licensure.** The experience gained between graduation and licensure is called *internship*.

In total, an MFT needs 3,000 hours of qualifying supervised experience to become eligible for MFT licensing exams. One key difference from the other mental health professions covered in this text is that MFTs can count experience gained during their graduate degree programs – up to 1,300 hours – toward the 3,000 total hours required for licensure.[33]

Practicum

The practicum is supervised experience obtained as part of the graduate degree program. Some universities have students complete their practicum at university-run clinics, while others partner with community agencies to place their students in the field for practicum. In either case, the school and the practicum site must have a written agreement that details how supervision is provided and ensures that the school will receive regular reports on the trainee's performance.[34]

California law requires MFT students to complete at least 225 hours of direct client contact during practicum, though up to 75 of these hours can be satisfied with "client-centered advocacy" (this term is defined specifically in the law; it essentially involves efforts to link

---

[33] California Business and Professions Code section 4980.43
[34] California Business and Professions Code section 4980.42(e)

clients with resources outside of a therapy session).[35] While in practicum, a student is considered to be an MFT Trainee, and they and their workplaces must refer to them as such.[36]

No student can begin seeing clients as part of practicum before they are enrolled in a practicum class. Once students have started the practicum, they must continue to be enrolled in practicum as long as they are seeing clients (the law allows for enrollment breaks of up to 90 days to account for gaps between quarters or semesters). When a student has completed their final academic term of practicum, they can continue completing their client contact hours so long as they complete all degree requirements (including hours) within 90 days of their last practicum enrollment.[37]

Students are, of course, required to be under supervision while in practicum. As you might expect, trainees need more supervision than interns do. The BBS considers one hour of individual supervision or two hours of group supervision, in a group of no more than eight total supervisees, to be one "unit" of supervision. Trainees are required to receive at least one unit of supervision in every week they gain experience for licensure. Over the total time a trainee is at a practicum site, the trainee must receive at least one unit of supervision for every five hours of client contact they completed at that site.[38]

Most trainees are not paid while completing their services, but there is nothing prohibiting payment. Trainees can be employees of a clinic or agency, or can work as volunteers. They cannot be utilized as independent contractors. Trainees also may not work in a private practice setting.[39]

Internship

Completion of the graduate degree and advancement to internship are major accomplishments for the aspiring MFT. As an MFT, the first time you submit paperwork to the BBS will likely be your application for intern registration. As long as you submit your

---

[35] California Business and Professions Code section 4980.36(d)(1)(B)(vi)
[36] California Business and Professions Code section 4980.42(a)
[37] California Business and Professions Code section 4980.42
[38] California Business and Professions Code section 4980.43(c)(1)
[39] California Business and Professions Code section 4980.43(d)(1)(C)

application for intern registration within 90 days of your degree posting date on your transcript, you can count any hours of experience gained between graduation and intern registration toward the 3,000 needed for licensure. Otherwise, any hours of experience gained in that gap between graduation and registration cannot be counted.[40]

As with MFT trainees, MFT interns can either be employed or work as volunteers, but cannot serve as independent contractors. Unlike MFT trainees, MFT registered interns can work in private practice settings.[41]

Once an MFT in training registers with the state as an MFT intern, they can keep that registration number for up to six years.[42] However, this does not mean that all licensure hours must be completed before those six years are up or else the MFT must completely start over. It is not unusual for an MFT intern who has taken time off to raise children, care for family members, or complete a tour of duty in the military to obtain a second intern registration number once their original number expires. When considering an application for license exam eligibility, the BBS will review the applicant's experience for the six years immediately before the application date – even if that experience was gained under two different intern registration numbers.[43] The only thing that changes with a second intern registration number is that the MFT intern can no longer work in a private practice setting.[44]

Like trainees, interns must receive at least one unit of supervision in each week they gain hours of clinical experience for licensure. Because they have completed their graduate education and gotten some supervised experience already, interns are considered by the law to need less supervision than trainees. Each week an intern gains experience for licensure, how much supervision the intern needs depends on how much client contact they had. **If the intern saw clients for 10 hours or fewer, one unit of supervision is all that is needed that week. If the intern saw clients for more than 10 hours, a second unit of supervision is necessary in the same**

---

[40] California Business and Professions Code section 4980.43(g)
[41] California Business and Professions Code section 4980.43(e)(2)
[42] California Business and Professions Code section 4984.01(c)
[43] California Business and Professions Code section 4980.43(a)(6)
[44] California Business and Professions Code section 4984.01(c)

week. There is no overall ratio that interns must meet in regard to their total time at an internship site.[45]

Who can supervise?

Unlike some other states, California does not require a prelicensed MFT to be supervised by an AAMFT Approved Supervisor. In fact, the MFT intern or trainee does not even need to be supervised by an LMFT. In order for a supervisor to be acceptable to the BBS, they must have been licensed in California as a Psychologist, Psychiatrist, LMFT, LCSW, or LPCC[46] for at least two years, and they must have taken at least a six-hour continuing education course on the supervision process. The supervisor must have provided counseling or supervision services for at least two years in the five years leading up to starting supervision with a new trainee or intern. In order for a supervisor to continue supervising, they must take at least six hours of continuing education on supervision in each two-year license renewal period.

If the supervisor is not an LMFT, the individual must at least have sufficient training, education, and experience in MFT to practice competently. The supervisor also must stay informed of developments in the MFT field, and changes in the laws that govern MFTs.[47]

A supervisor cannot supervise someone who was their therapy client at any point in the past.[48] Any hours of experience earned under a supervisor who is the supervisee's spouse, relative, or domestic partner, or a supervisor will not be counted toward licensure.[49] The BBS also will not count any hours gained under a supervisor who the intern or trainee has had a prior personal or business relationship that undermines the authority or effectiveness of supervision.

---

[45] California Business and Professions Code section 4980.43(c)
[46] LPCCs must complete additional training and supervised experience to supervise MFT interns and trainees. These additional requirements are the same as those for an LPCC to work with couples and families specified in the chapter on Scope of Practice.
[47] California Code of Regulations title 16 section 1833.1(a)(2) and (3)
[48] California Business and Professions Code section 4980.03(g)(3)
[49] California Code of Regulations title 16 section 1833(b)(3)

Specific areas of experience

The requirements for types of supervised experience leading to LMFT licensure are defined in Table 2.1. As you can see, there are many minimums and maximums to which MFTs must adhere.

Additional minimums and maximums

In addition to the requirements in Table 2.1, several other limits on experience leading to LMFT licensure apply:[50]

- The 3,000 hours of experience must be gained over at least a total of 104 weeks (two years). At least 52 of those weeks must include at least one hour of individual supervision.
- No more than 40 total hours may be gained in any given week.
- No more than 6 hours of supervision will be credited in any given week.[51]
- Pre-degree hours from all categories may not total more than 1,300 hours.
- Pre-degree psychotherapy (all categories) and supervision may not total more than 750 hours.

---

[50] California Business and Professions Code section 4980.43 and California Code of Regulations title 16 section 1833

[51] This limit was raised from five hours to six as of January 1, 2015. See California Business and Professions Code section 4980.43(c)(1), (2), and (8). The change applies retroactively, to supervision gained on or after January 1, 2009. So if you have worked at multiple settings and were getting more than five hours of supervision a week, you may want to revise your experience forms to include additional supervision hours you actually attended but previously could not count toward licensure.

Table 2.1: Supervised experience for LMFT licensure

Category	Minimum/maximum[52]	
Individual psychotherapy	**No minimum or maximum.**	
Couple, family, and child psychotherapy	**Minimum 500 hours.** Up to 150 hours of couple and family (that is, *not* individual child) psychotherapy are double-counted toward the 3,000 total hours required for licensure.	
Group therapy	**Maximum 500 hours.**	
Telephone and Internet counseling	**Maximum 375 hours.** Note that you generally may not counsel clients outside of California (see Chapter 1, Scope of Practice).	
Client-centered advocacy	**Combined maximum 500 hours** for these two categories. "Client-centered advocacy" involves efforts to link clients with resources outside of a therapy session.	
Writing clinical reports, administering tests, and writing notes		
Supervision	Part of a combined maximum. →	
Workshops, trainings, and seminars	**Maximum 250 hours.** For agency in-service and similar trainings, it is at the discretion of the supervisor what will qualify within this category.	**Combined maximum 1,000 hours** for these three categories.
Personal psychotherapy (when the applicant is the client)	**Maximum 100 hours.** These hours are triple-counted, for a total of up to 300 hours of credit toward the 3,000 total supervised hours required for licensure.	

[52] California Business and Professions Code section 4980.43 and California Code of Regulations title 16 section 1833

Supervisors have some discretion in what will qualify under specific types of experience. For example, supervisors determine what is appropriate within the category of "Workshops, trainings, and seminars." In addition, hours of experience with individual children can either be counted as individual psychotherapy or within the "Couple, family, and child psychotherapy" category.

Note that some of these rules changed in January 2012. For guidance on minimums and maximums that apply to experience gained before January 1, 2012, consult the BBS web site.[53]

Proposed changes

As mentioned at the beginning of this chapter, the road to licensure for MFTs is not as swift as it would at first appear to be. While 3,000 hours is generally understood to be the equivalent of two years of full-time supervised practice, the average California MFT takes more than four years to get from graduation to their licensing exams. This is despite the fact that up to 1,300 hours of experience can be credited from within the degree program.

The professional associations in the state (AAMFT-CA and CAMFT) engaged in a joint effort in 2014 to learn more about the reasons for these delays and how the licensure process could be streamlined without coming at the expense of public safety. AAMFT-CA developed a white paper on the difficulties MFTs have in getting licensed in California, which they have made publicly available.[54] The BBS, through its Supervision Committee, examined these findings alongside draft legislative language put together by CAMFT, and agreed to sponsor legislation largely along the lines of what the associations were asking for.[55]

The bill proposed by the BBS would make the experience requirements for LMFTs much more similar to the current

---

[53] www.bbs.ca.gov
[54] Caldwell, B. E., Loewy, O., Kahn, A. C., Tobie, C., & Dunham, Z. (2014). *Challenges in MFT licensing in California.* Santa Barbara, CA: AAMFT-CA. Available online at aamftca.org/wp-content/uploads/2014/10/White-Paper-Challenges-in-MFT-licensing-in-California-2014.pdf
[55] Materials for the November 19-20, 2014 meeting of the Board of Behavioral Sciences (pages 45-64)

requirements for LCSWs. While LMFTs would still need a total of 3,000 hours of supervised experience, and it would still be possible to count up to 1,300 pre-degree hours, many of the current minimums and maximums would go away, replaced with a simpler two-category structure: MFTs would need at least 1,750 client contact hours (including at least 500 hours with couples, families, and children), and could receive credit for up to 1,250 non-clinical hours. This second category would include things like supervision, client-centered advocacy, and other types of experience that currently are credited toward licensure but do not involve direct contact with clients.

The triple-counting of personal psychotherapy hours would go away, as these hours could not be counted at all. However, it is important to understand that neither the BBS nor the associations are saying such work has no value for new professionals; it can be critically important to your personal and professional growth to go to therapy. The legislative proposal merely fixes a longstanding problem with crediting those hours for licensure: They aren't accepted in other states, raising problems when it comes to portability. Personal psychotherapy also doesn't prepare you for licensing exams in the way that other forms of experience do, since there will not be any questions on the exams about your own experience as a client.

In order to ensure that those close to the end of their supervised experience aren't in any way disadvantaged by the changes, the BBS is proposing a two-year phase-in period (proposed to be the 2016 and 2017 calendar years). During that time, MFTs could apply for licensing exam eligibility under *either* set of standards, new or old. Those applying for exam eligibility on January 1, 2018 or later would need to do so under the new standards.

Ultimately, the BBS proposal is likely to offer a great deal of benefit to the overwhelming majority of MFT interns if it is adopted as proposed. Of course, at press time for this book, the proposal is just that: A proposal. Proposed laws often change significantly as they make their way through the state legislature, so it remains to be seen whether the idea will even become law at all, and if so, what it will look like in its final form.

Exams

California currently requires two examinations for MFT licensure. They must be taken in sequence, and neither can be taken until an MFT intern has completed their 3,000 required hours of supervised experience and been declared eligible to take the exams by the BBS. Note that the examination process for all BBS licensees changes significantly on January 1, 2016; see below for more on this. The BBS has a wealth of exam-related information on their web site, including candidate handbooks for both exams.

MFT Standard Written Exam

The MFT Standard Written Exam (SWE) is the first exam an applicant takes. It consists of a minimum of 175 multiple-choice questions, administered via computer in one of several testing centers around the state. (The exam may contain as many as 25 additional non-scored items that are being tested for possible inclusion as scoring items in later exams. These do not impact your results, but you do not know which items are non-scoring.) Once you start the test, you have 4 hours to complete it.[56]

The content of the SWE breaks down into the following categories (Table 2.2). As you can see, legal and ethical items make up fully a third of the test:

---

[56] PSI licensure:certification (2010). *Marriage and Family Therapist Standard Written Exam Candidate Handbook*. Las Vegas, NV: PSI.

Table 2.2: MFT Standard Written Exam content

Category	Percent of items
Clinical evaluation	22%
Crisis	14%
Treatment planning	14%
Treatment	17%
Ethics	16%
Law	17%

MFT Written Clinical Vignette

The MFT Written Clinical Vignette (WCV) exam can only be attempted after you have successfully passed the SWE. It is a vignette-based test, which means you will be given a paragraph-long case vignette that will apply to about 4-7 questions. The total exam consists of roughly 5-7 vignettes and a total of 30 questions. As with the SWE, you may also be given up to 10 nonscoring items, likely divided between two vignettes, that are being tested for possible inclusion in later exams. You have two hours to complete the test.[57]

The content of the WCV breaks down into the same categories as the SWE, but the candidate handbook for this exam does not give a breakdown of how the items are distributed proportionally across categories.

In most cases, you learn your results on both tests immediately. When you pass the SWE, you can quickly schedule your WCV exam. Once you have passed the WCV, there is a final round of paperwork (and a check) to file with the BBS before they issue your license number.

---

[57] PSI licensure:certification (2010). *Marriage and Family Therapist Written Clinical Vignette Exam Candidate Handbook*. Las Vegas, NV: PSI.

2016 changes in the exam process

Legislation passed in 2011 and revised in 2012 and 2013 will significantly change the testing process for LMFTs starting January 1, 2016.[58] Under the new testing structure, an MFT Intern will be required to take an exam on California Law and Ethics in their first year of intern registration.[59] If they pass the exam, they will not need to take another test until they have completed the rest of their supervised experience – at which point they will take a single clinical exam.

If the MFT intern fails the California Law and Ethics exam, they will need to take a 12-hour CE course in California Law and Ethics in order to renew their intern registration.[60] Once their registration renews, they will repeat the process – again needing to take the Law and Ethics exam and needing to take another CE course if they again fail. This process can be repeated as many times as it takes for the intern to pass the Law and Ethics test, up to the six-year maximum length of intern registration.

The new clinical exam that takes effect in 2016 will cover a combination of the topics currently covered in the two exams MFTs must take. The test will still be multiple-choice and administered via computer, and will include vignette-based items like those currently on the WCV exam in addition to straightforward multiple-choice questions.

The combined clinical test is expected to look very similar to the National MFT Exam, which is utilized for MFT licensure in every state except California. The BBS has been working collaboratively with the Association of Marriage and Family Therapy Regulatory Boards[61] (the group behind the national exam) to determine whether California may be able to transition to the National MFT Exam.

---

[58] SB704 (2011), SB1527 (2012), SB821 (2013)
[59] California Business and Professions Code section 4980.399
[60] California Business and Professions Code section 4980.399(d)
[61] www.amftrb.org

▶ Professional Clinical Counselors

> **To become an LPCC, you need a qualifying graduate degree, 3,000 hours of *postdegree* supervised experience, and passing scores on the California Law and Ethics Exam and the National Clinical Mental Health Counseling Exam.** The testing process will change in 2016.

The LPCC license is California's newest mental health license. The LPCC licensing law was passed in 2009 and the normal licensure process began in 2012. The licensing requirements for LPCCs were derived largely from two sources: The educational requirements of the Commission on Accreditation for Counseling and Related Educational Programs (to ensure that educational standards were consistent with other states), and the experience requirements of LMFTs (to ensure that the licenses would have comparable experience).

Education

California's curriculum requirements for graduate degrees leading to LPCC licensure are drawn largely from the Core Content areas required by the Council for Accreditation of Counseling and Related Educational Programs (CACREP). However, California also adds a number of specific requirements on to the CACREP standards. For example, California requires a master's or doctoral degree of at least 60 semester units (90 quarter units), while many other states require 48 or fewer. California also requires specific course content not required by CACREP. If you are currently studying outside of California but wish to eventually license as an LPCC within California, it is vital that you make sure your degree program will meet California's requirements.[62] The BBS does allow some deficiencies to

---

[62] California's standards for graduate education leading to LPCC licensure changed significantly for students beginning their education on or after August 1, 2012. The discussion here is based on the new, more stringent requirements. Those who began their degrees earlier than August 2012 can qualify under the old requirements as long as they complete their degrees by

be made up when applicants come to California from out of state, but you ultimately will need to meet all of the California standards.

Graduate degree content

Counseling degrees can carry a variety of different titles. Degrees for LPCCs are evaluated on their content and not their name.[63] Your master's or doctoral degree must be at least 60 semester units (90 quarter units) in total, and must include at least three semester units (4.5 quarter units) in each of the following to be a qualifying degree for LPCC licensure. Note that within each of these courses are more specific content requirements spelled out in the law:[64]

- Theory and technique of counseling and psychotherapy
- Development across the life span
- Career counseling
- Group counseling
- Testing and assessment measures
- Multicultural counseling
- Diagnosis
- Research and evaluation
- California law and ethics
- Psychopharmacology
- Addiction counseling
- Crisis and trauma counseling

If your degree is lacking in up to three of these areas, it is possible to make up the missing pieces through postdegree education. Any classes you take to make up for deficiencies in your degree must be at an accredited or approved graduate school, and must be at least three semester units (4.5 quarter units).[65]

2018. Some schools adopted the new requirements early, so check with your university if you are unsure which set of requirements applies to you.
[63] California Business and Professions Code section 4999.33(b)
[64] California Business and Professions Code section 4999.33(c)(1)
[65] California Business and Professions Code section 4999.33(f)

The qualifying degree must also include at least 15 semester units (22.5 quarter units) in advanced coursework, focused on specific populations or treatment issues.[66] It must also include at least six semester units (nine quarter units) of practicum, which is further discussed in Supervised Experience below.[67]

There are several additional content areas that must be included in a qualifying graduate degree, though they do not require separate courses; they simply must be included somewhere in the curriculum within a credit-level class:[68]

- Human behavior within the context of socioeconomic status and other contextual factors
- Human behavior within the social context of a variety of California cultures
- Cultural competency and sensitivity
- Understanding of the impact of socioeconomic status on available treatment and resources
- Multicultural development and cross-cultural interaction, and how these impact therapy
- Human sexuality
- Intimate partner violence assessment and intervention
- Child abuse assessment and reporting
- Aging and long-term care, including assessment and reporting of abuse

A qualifying degree leading to LPCC licensure must also include instruction in California's public mental health system, including information about recovery-oriented care and opportunities to meet with public mental health consumers and family members.[69]

Finally, the law requires that these additional content areas be included in a qualifying degree, though they do not need to be within

---

[66] California Business and Professions Code section 4999.33(c)(2)
[67] California Business and Professions Code section 4999.33(c)(3)
[68] California Business and Professions Code section 4999.33(d)
[69] California Business and Professions Code section 4999.33(e)

credit-level coursework. They can be delivered in workshops or other formats that do not lead to course credit:[70]

- Case management
- Systems of care for the severely mentally ill
- Public and private services and supports available for the severely mentally ill
- Community resources for persons with mental illness and for victims of abuse
- Disaster and trauma response
- Advocacy for the severely mentally ill
- Collaborative treatment

Supervised Experience

PCCs begin seeing clients during their graduate degree programs. **When a student is completing required hours of clinical experience as part of their graduate degree, they are considered to be a PCC Trainee.** The experience they are completing is called a *practicum*. **Once they graduate, the PCC-in-training applies to the BBS to become a Professional Clinical Counselor Registered Intern until they move ahead to licensure.** The experience gained between graduation and licensure is called *internship*.

In total, a PCC needs 3,280 hours of qualifying supervised experience to become eligible for their licensing exams: 280 hours of client contact during the practicum, and 3,000 additional hours of qualifying experience as an intern.[71] None of the experience gained as a trainee can count toward the 3,000 hours required after the degree.[72]

---

[70] California Business and Professions Code section 4999.33(d)(6)
[71] California Business and Professions Code sections 4999.33(c)(3)(K) and 4999.46(b)
[72] California Business and Professions Code section 4999.36(e)

Practicum

The practicum is supervised experience obtained as part of the graduate degree program. Some universities have students complete their practicum at university-run clinics, while others partner with community agencies to place their students in the field for practicum. In either case, the school and the practicum site must have a written agreement that details how supervision is provided and ensures that the school will receive regular reports on the trainee's performance.[73]

California law requires PCC students to complete at least 280 hours of direct client contact during practicum. While in practicum, a student is considered to be a Clinical Counselor Trainee, and they and their workplaces must refer to them as such.[74]

Students are, of course, required to be under supervision while in practicum. As you might expect, trainees need more supervision than interns do. The BBS considers one hour of individual supervision or two hours of group supervision, in a group of no more than eight total supervisees, to be one "unit" of supervision. Trainees are required to receive at least one unit of supervision in every week they gain experience for licensure. Over the total time a trainee is at a practicum site, the trainee must receive at least one unit of supervision for every five hours of client contact they completed at that site.[75]

Most trainees are not paid while completing their services, but there is nothing prohibiting payment. Trainees can be employees of a clinic or agency, or can work as volunteers. They cannot be utilized as independent contractors. Trainees also may not work in a private practice setting.[76]

Internship

Completion of the graduate degree and advancement to internship are major accomplishments for the developing PCC. As a PCC, the first time you submit paperwork to the BBS will likely be your application for intern registration. As long as you submit your

---

[73] California Business and Professions Code section 4999.36(b)
[74] California Business and Professions Code section 4999.36(a)
[75] California Business and Professions Code section 4999.36(f)
[76] California Business and Professions Code section 4999.34(c)

application for intern registration within 90 days of your degree posting date on your transcript, you can count any hours of experience gained between graduation and intern registration toward the 3,000 postdegree hours needed for licensure. Otherwise, any hours of experience gained in that gap between graduation and registration cannot be counted.[77]

As with clinical counselor trainees, PCC interns can either be employed or work as volunteers, but cannot serve as independent contractors. Unlike clinical counselor trainees, PCC registered interns can work in private practice settings.[78]

Once a PCC in training registers with the state as an intern, they can keep that registration number for up to six years.[79] This does not mean that all licensure hours must be completed before those six years are up or else the PCC must completely start over – it is not unusual for a PCC Intern who has taken time off to raise children, care for family members, or complete a tour of duty in the military to obtain a second intern registration number once their original number expires. Still, there is reason to try to avoid this. The law requires that anyone applying for a second PCC intern registration number must have met the educational requirements in place *at the time of the second application*.[80] If the educational requirements had changed at all in the previous six years, the intern would need to take additional coursework to meet the new standards. In addition, an intern working under their second intern registration cannot work in a private practice.[81]

When considering an application for license exam eligibility, the BBS will review the applicant's experience for the six years immediately before the application date – even if that experience was gained under two different intern registration numbers.[82]

Like trainees, interns must receive at least one unit of supervision in each week they gain hours of clinical experience for licensure. Because they have completed their graduate education and

---

[77] California Business and Professions Code section 4999.46(d)
[78] California Business and Professions Code section 4999.45(a)(2)
[79] California Business and Professions Code section 4999.45(a)(4)
[80] California Business and Professions Code section 4999.45(b)
[81] California Business and Professions Code section 4999.45(b)
[82] California Business and Professions Code section 4999.46(c)

gotten some supervised experience already, interns are considered by the law to need less supervision than trainees. Each week an intern gains experience for licensure, how much supervision the intern needs depends on how much client contact they had. **If the intern saw clients for 10 hours or fewer, one unit of supervision is all that is needed that week. If the intern saw clients for more than 10 hours, a second unit of supervision is necessary in the same week.** There is no overall ratio that interns must meet in regard to their total time at an internship site.[83]

Who can supervise?

A clinical counseling intern or trainee can be supervised in California by a Psychologist, Psychiatrist, LMFT, LCSW, or LPCC who has been licensed in the state for at least two years and has taken at least a six-hour continuing education course on the supervision process.[84] The supervisor must have provided counseling or supervision services for at least two years in the five years leading up to starting supervision with a new trainee or intern. In order for a supervisor to continue supervising, they must take at least six hours of continuing education on supervision in each two-year license renewal period.

If the supervisor is not an LPCC, the individual must at least have sufficient training, education, and experience in professional clinical counseling to practice competently. The supervisor also must stay informed of developments in the PCC field, and changes in the laws that govern LPCCs.[85]

Recall from the earlier discussion of scope of practice (chapter 1) that PCCs cannot assess or treat couples or families unless they have fulfilled additional requirements for education and supervised experience. When a PCC (regardless of licensure status) is gaining their supervised experience in couple, family, and child work to comply with these requirements, they must be supervised by either an

---

[83] California Business and Professions Code section 4999.46(g)
[84] California Code of Regulations title 16 section 1821(b)
[85] California Code of Regulations title 16 section 1821(b)

LMFT or by an LPCC who has already met the requirements to work independently with couples and families.[86]

Any hours of experience earned under a supervisor who is the supervisee's spouse or relative (by blood or marriage) will not be counted toward licensure.[87] The BBS also will not count any hours gained under a supervisor who the intern or trainee has had a prior personal or business relationship that undermines the authority or effectiveness of supervision.

The supervision plan

PCC interns must work with their supervisors to develop a supervision plan for each work setting, detailing the goals and objectives of supervision. The supervision plan must be submitted to the BBS when the associate applies for licensure.[88]

Specific areas of experience

The supervised experience requirements for LPCC licensure are summarized in Table 2.3.

Additional minimums and maximums

In addition to the requirements in Table 2.3, a few other limits on experience leading to LPCC licensure apply:[89]

- The 3,000 hours of experience must be gained over at least a total of 104 weeks (two years). At least 52 of those weeks must include at least one hour of individual supervision.
- No more than 40 total hours may be gained in any given week.
- No more than 6 hours of supervision will be credited in any given week.[90]

---

[86] California Code of Regulations title 16 section 1820.5
[87] California Code of Regulations title 16 section 1833(b)(3)
[88] California Code of Regulations title 16 section 1822(b)
[89] California Business and Professions Code section 4999.46 and California Code of Regulations title 16 section 1820(e)

Table 2.3: Supervised experience for LPCC licensure[91]

Category	Minimum/maximum	
Individual or group counseling	**Minimum 1,750 hours,** including a maximum **of 500 hours** of group counseling and a minimum **of 150 hours** in a hospital or community mental health setting.	
Counseling via telehealth	Maximum **375 hours.** Note that you generally may not counsel clients outside of California (see Chapter 1, Scope of Practice).	
Supervision	Part of combined maximum →	
Client-centered advocacy	This category involves efforts to link clients with resources outside of a therapy session.	Maximum **1,250 hours** in these four categories combined.
Testing, writing clinical reports, and writing notes	Maximum **250 hours.**	
Workshops, trainings, and seminars	Maximum **250 hours.**	

[90] This limit was raised from five hours to six as of January 1, 2015. See California Business and Professions Code section 4999.46(g)(1). The change applies retroactively, to supervision gained on or after January 1, 2009. So if you have worked at multiple settings and were getting more than five hours of supervision a week, you may want to revise your experience forms to include additional supervision hours you actually attended but previously could not count toward licensure.

[91] California Business and Professions Code section 4999.46

Supervisors have some discretion in what will qualify under specific types of experience. For example, supervisors determine what is appropriate within the category of "Workshops, trainings, and seminars."

Proposed changes

The BBS has proposed changes in the PCC licensing requirements that would do away with some of the maximums for specific types of experience. In their place would be a structure most similar to the current licensing structure for clinical social workers. In order to qualify for licensure, PCCs would need at least 3,000 hours of experience, consisting of at least 1,750 hours of clinical experience and no more than 1,250 hours of non-clinical experience. Current maximums in the *Workshops, trainings, and seminars* and *Testing, writing clinical reports, and writing notes* categories would be eliminated.[92] The California Association of LPCCs requested that the 150-hour minimum in a hospital or community mental health setting be kept.

In order to ensure that those close to the end of their supervised experience aren't in any way disadvantaged by the changes, the BBS is proposing a two-year phase-in period (proposed to be the 2016 and 2017 calendar years). During that time, PCCs could apply for licensing exam eligibility under *either* set of standards, new or old. Those applying for exam eligibility on January 1, 2018 or later would need to do so under the new standards.

It is important to remember that, at press time for this book, the BBS proposal was just that: A proposal. Proposed laws often change significantly as they make their way through the state legislature, so it remains to be seen whether the idea will even become law at all, and if so, what it will look like in its final form.

---

[92] Materials for the November 19-20, 2014 meeting of the Board of Behavioral Sciences (pages 45-64)

Exams

California currently requires two examinations for LPCC licensure. They must be taken in sequence, and neither can be taken until a PCC intern has completed their 3,000 required hours of supervised postdegree experience and been declared eligible to take the exams by the BBS.

California Law and Ethics Exam

The California Law and Ethics Exam consists of at least 100 multiple-choice questions on the laws and ethical rules that govern the profession of clinical counseling in California. It is administered via computer in one of several testing centers around the state. (The exam may contain as many as 50 additional non-scored items that are being tested for possible inclusion as scoring items in later exams. These do not impact your results, but you do not know which items are nonscoring.) Once you start the test, you have 90 minutes to complete it.[93]

National Clinical Mental Health Counseling Exam

California recognizes the National Clinical Mental Health Counseling Exam (NCMHCE) as the clinical examination for licensure as an LPCC. This exam, which is developed by the National Board for Certified Counselors, consists of 10 case vignettes that assess a counselor's ability to gather necessary information and make appropriate clinical decisions. Each case is divided into five to eight sections. Some questions accept multiple responses, while others ask the examinee to choose a single best option from the choices presented.[94] Unlike the California exams in the other professions,

---

[93] PSI licensure:certification (2011). *Licensed Professional Clinical Counselors Jurisprudence & Ethics Written Examination Candidate Handbook.* Las Vegas, NV: PSI.

[94] National Board for Certified Counselors (2005). *Candidate Handbook for State Credentialing.* Greensboro, NC: NBCC.

scores on the NCMHCE are not available immediately; they take approximately six weeks to process.[95]

2016 changes in the exam process

Legislation passed in 2011 and revised in 2012 and 2013 will significantly change the testing process for LPCCs starting January 1, 2016.[96] Under the new testing structure, a PCC Intern will be required to take an exam on California Law and Ethics in their first year of intern registration. If they pass the exam, they will not need to take another test until they have completed the rest of their supervised experience – at which point they will take a single clinical exam (the national exam described above).

If the PCC intern fails the California Law and Ethics exam, they will need to take a 12-hour CE course in California Law and Ethics in order to renew their intern registration. Once their registration renews, they will repeat the process, again needing to take the Law and Ethics exam and needing to take another CE course if they again fail. This process can be repeated as many times as it takes for the intern to pass the law and ethics test, up to the six-year maximum length of intern registration. A PCC intern must pass the law and ethics exam to qualify for a second intern registration number.

---

[95] National Board for Certified Counselors: National Clinical Mental Health Counseling Examination (NCMHCE)
[96] SB704 (2011), SB1527 (2012), SB821 (2013)

▶ Clinical Social Workers

> **To become an LCSW, you need a qualifying graduate degree, 3,200 hours of supervised experience, and passing scores on California's Standard Written Exam and Written Clinical Vignette exam.** The testing process will change significantly in 2016.

Of the three professions covered in this text, Clinical Social Workers have the fewest licensure requirements spelled out in state law. This is because the state has largely deferred to national standards in the clinical social work profession, relying on national accreditation standards for graduate education and, as of 2016, the national social work exam.

Education

Clinical social workers must possess a master's degree from an accredited school of social work.[97] The Council on Social Work Education (CSWE) is the national accrediting body for social work programs, and as of December 2014, it recognized 23 master's degree programs in California as accredited.[98]

The social worker must also have training in the following areas, though these can be either within the degree program or taken separately.[99] Note that state law includes more specific content requirements within some of these training areas:

- Chemical dependency
- Intimate partner violence assessment and intervention (minimum 15 contact hours)
- Human sexuality (minimum 10 hours)
- Child abuse assessment and reporting (minimum 7 hours)

---

[97] California Business and Professions Code section 4996.2(b)
[98] CSWE Directory of Accredited Programs
[99] California Business and Professions Code section 4996.2

Supervised postdegree experience

Completion of the graduate degree and advancement to internship are major accomplishments for the developing CSW. Once a social worker has completed their degree, they must register with the BBS as an Associate Clinical Social Worker. This registration is necessary before gaining any of the required postdegree supervised experience for licensure.[100]

In total, a CSW needs 3,200 hours of qualifying postdegree supervised experience to become eligible for CSW licensing exams. This does not include any experience gained as part of the degree. Of those 3,200 hours, at least 1,700 must be supervised by an LCSW (more on this below).[101] Like members of the other mental health professions who have completed their degrees and are gathering hours of experience toward licensure, Associate CSWs are allowed to work in private practice settings.[102]

Once a person registers with the state as an associate CSW, they can keep that registration number for up to six years.[103] However, this does not mean that all licensure hours must be completed before that six years are up or else the associate must completely start over. It is not unusual for an Associate CSW who has taken time off to raise children, care for family members, or complete a tour of duty in the military to obtain a second registration number once their original number expires. When considering an application for license exam eligibility, the BBS will review the applicant's experience for the six years immediately before the application date – even if that experience was gained under two different registration numbers.[104] The only thing that changes with a second registration number is that the Associate CSW can no longer work in a private practice setting.[105]

Associate CSWs must receive at least one hour of direct supervisor contact in each week they gain experience toward

---

[100] California Business and Professions Code section 4996.18
[101] California Business and Professions Code section 4996.23(a)
[102] California Business and Professions Code section 4996.23(g)
[103] California Business and Professions Code section 4996.28(b)
[104] California Business and Professions Code section 4996.23(a)(4)
[105] California Business and Professions Code section 4996.28(b)

licensure.[106] One hour of individual supervision or two hours of group supervision in a group of no more than eight supervisees is considered an "hour of direct supervisor contact" in BBS language,[107] which admittedly can get confusing. Each week an associate sees clients for more than 10 hours, they need to receive a second hour of direct supervisor contact.[108]

Who can supervise?

Unlike the other masters-level mental health professions in California, social workers are required to have some of their supervised experience under someone holding the same license they seek. As mentioned above, 1,700 hours of experience for an Associate CSW must be supervised by an LCSW. The remainder of the experience can be supervised by a licensed Psychologist, Psychiatrist, LMFT, LCSW, or LPCC who has taken at least a 15-hour continuing education course on the supervision process, including specific content requirements.[109] Regardless of licensure type, anyone supervising an ACSW must have been licensed for at least two years.[110] The supervisor must have provided counseling or supervision services for at least two years in the five years leading up to starting supervision with a new associate.[111]

The supervision plan

Associate CSWs must work with their supervisors to develop a supervision plan for each work setting, detailing the goals of supervision. These goals have to include ongoing assessment of the associate's strengths and weaknesses, and work to ensure practice in keeping with legal requirements. Supervisors and associates can add to this whatever goals they wish, presuming they are appropriate goals

---

[106] California Business and Professions Code section 4996.23(n)
[107] California Business and Professions Code section 4996.23(c)(2)
[108] California Business and Professions Code section 4996.23(c)(3)
[109] California Code of Regulations title 16 sections 1870(a)(4)(A) and 1874
[110] California Code of Regulations title 16 section 1870(a)(2)
[111] California Code of Regulations title 16 section 1870(a)(3)

for supervision. The supervision plan must be submitted to the BBS when the associate applies for licensure.[112]

Specific areas of experience

The requirements for specific supervised experience leading to LCSW licensure are defined in Table 2.4. As you can see, it is much simpler than the experience requirements for LPCCs and LMFTs.

Additional minimums and maximums

In addition to the requirements in the chart above, several other limits on experience leading to LCSW licensure apply:

- The 3,200 hours of experience must be gained over at least a total of 104 weeks (two years). At least 52 of those weeks must include at least one hour of individual supervision. Of the 52 weeks of individual supervision, at least 13 weeks must be under the supervision of an LCSW.[113]
- No more than 40 total hours may be gained in a week.[114]
- No more than 5 hours of supervision will be credited in any given week.[115]

---

[112] California Business and Professions Code section 4996.23(d)
[113] California Business and Professions Code section 4996.23(a)(4) and (c)(5)
[114] California Business and Professions Code section 4996.23(a)(5)
[115] California Business and Professions Code section 4996.23(c)(3)

Table 2.4: Supervised experience for LCSW licensure

Category	Minimum/maximum[116]
Clinical psychosocial assessment, diagnosis, and treatment, including therapy or counseling	**Minimum 2,000 hours,** including a minimum **of 750 hours providing individual or group psychotherapy**
Client-centered advocacy, consultation, evaluation, and research	**Minimum 1,200 hours.**

Exams

California currently requires two examinations for LCSW licensure. They must be taken in sequence, and neither can be taken until an Associate CSW has completed their 3,200 required hours of supervised postdegree experience and been declared eligible to take the exams by the BBS. Note that the examination process for all BBS licensees changes significantly on January 1, 2016; see below for more on this. The BBS has a wealth of exam-related information on their web site, including candidate handbooks for both exams.

CSW Standard Written Exam

The CSW Standard Written Exam (SWE) is the first exam an applicant takes. It consists of a minimum of 175 multiple-choice questions, administered via computer in one of several testing centers around the state. (The exam may contain as many as 25 additional nonscored items that are being tested for possible inclusion as scoring items in later exams. These do not impact your results, but you do not know which items are nonscoring.) Once you start the test, you have 4 hours to complete it.[117]

---

[116] California Business and Professions Code section 4996.23(a)
[117] PSI licensure:certification (2010). *Licensed Clinical Social Worker Standard Written Exam Candidate Handbook.* Las Vegas, NV: PSI.

The content of the SWE breaks down into the following categories. As you can see, assessment and diagnosis combine to make up fully a third of the test, while interventions make up another third:

Table 2.5: CSW Standard Written Exam content

Category	Percent of items
Biopsychosocial assessment	27%
Diagnostic formulation	6%
Treatment planning	11%
Resource coordination	5%
Therapeutic interventions	33%
Law	9%
Ethics	9%

CSW Written Clinical Vignette

The CSW Written Clinical Vignette (WCV) exam can only be attempted after you have successfully passed the SWE. It is a vignette-based test, which means you will be given a paragraph-long case vignette that will apply to about 4-7 questions. The total exam consists of roughly 5-7 vignettes and a total of 30 questions. As with the SWE, you may also be given up to 10 nonscoring items, likely divided between two vignettes, that are being tested for possible inclusion in later exams. You have two hours to complete the test.[118]

The content of the WCV breaks down into the same categories as the SWE, but the candidate handbook for this exam notes that the proportions of items in each category will vary from one exam cycle to the next.

In most cases, you learn your results on both tests immediately. When you pass the SWE, you can quickly schedule your

---

[118] PSI licensure:certification (2010). *Licensed Clinical Social Worker Written Clinical Vignette Exam Candidate Handbook.* Las Vegas, NV: PSI.

WCV exam. Once you have passed the WCV, there is a final round of paperwork (and a check) to file with the BBS before they issue your license number.

2016 changes in the exam process

Legislation passed in 2011 and revised in 2012 and 2013 will significantly change the testing process for CSWs starting January 1, 2016.[119] Under the new testing structure, an Associate CSW will be required to take an **exam on California Law and Ethics** in their first year of associate registration.[120] If they pass the exam, they will not need to take another test until they have completed their supervised experience – at which point they will take a single **clinical exam**.

If the Associate CSW fails the California Law and Ethics exam, they will need to take a 12-hour CE course in California Law and Ethics in order to renew their registration.[121] Once their registration renews, they will repeat the process, again needing to take the Law and Ethics exam and, if they fail, needing to take another CE course to renew the registration. This process can be repeated as many times as it takes for the associate to pass the Law and Ethics test, up to the six-year maximum length of registration.

Social workers will also enjoy another important change as of January 1, 2016: The clinical exam for CSWs will change from being a state-based exam to being the ASWB Clinical Level Exam (the national exam for CSWs).

---

[119] 2011 legislation: SB704 (2011), SB1527 (2012), SB821 (2013)
[120] California Business and Professions Code section 4992.05
[121] California Business and Professions Code section 4992.09

3

Unprofessional Conduct

The previous chapter focused on what you need to do to become a Marriage and Family Therapist, Professional Clinical Counselor, or Clinical Social Worker. This chapter focuses on state laws regarding what you need to do – or, in many cases, what you need to avoid doing – once you are in the mental health professions. Any act that qualifies as "Unprofessional Conduct" in state law can lead to action against your license or registration. As we will see, unprofessional conduct is not limited to what happens inside the therapy room; trouble with the law in any other area of life can also impact the BBS' view of whether you are a good fit for your profession. Thankfully, there are some common-sense steps you can take to protect yourself and your license or registration.

▶ The meaning of "unprofessional conduct"

When you enter into the role of an LMFT, LPCC, or LCSW, you are voluntarily giving up some of your legal rights and agreeing to be held to a higher standard of behavior than the ordinary person. As one example of the rights you give up, consider freedom of speech, one of our fundamental First Amendment rights in the United States. As an LMFT, LPCC, or LCSW, you agree to limit your freedom of speech when it comes to discussing what happens in your office. If you choose to exercise what would, for a normal person, be freedom of speech and reveal who your clients are to the world, you could lose your license to practice.

This is important to consider if you are early in your education as a mental health professional. One of the most controversial policy areas in the mental health field right now is whether a therapist also gives up their freedom to practice religion as they see fit within the context of their licensed mental health work. Several recent lawsuits have focused on therapists or students who refused to treat gay or lesbian clients, citing their religious beliefs.[122] Does a client's right to receive competent services regardless of their sexual orientation trump a therapist's right to act in accordance with their religious beliefs while working under their state license?

Unfortunately, the resolution of those lawsuits did little to clarify the limits of religious practice for mental health professionals.[123] What is clear is that mental health professionals operate in an area of public trust, bestowed upon us in the form of state licensure. In exchange, we agree to uphold a high standard of professional behavior that most people – even most professionals – do not need to follow.

---

[122] Caldwell, B. E. (2011). The dilemma: Can a religious therapist refuse to treat gay and lesbian clients? *Family Therapy Magazine, 10*(5), 50-52. AAMFT was kind enough to allow me to reprint the article in full on my blog: www.psychotherapynotes.com/uncategorized/can-a-religious-therapist-refuse-to-treat-gay-and-lesbian-clients/

[123] I wrote on the resolution of two key cases here: www.psychotherapynotes.com/education-2/eastern-michigan-settles-julea-ward-case/

Why the statutes exist

As is the case with any established higher standards of behavior, there will be some within the mental health professions who violate those standards. Unprofessional conduct statutes give the state the authority to discipline the licenses of those who violate accepted standards of professional behavior. For less severe violations, punishments such as probation are often sufficient. For severe or repeat violations of professional standards, the unprofessional conduct statutes allow the BBS to suspend or even revoke a practitioner's license.

It benefits the professions as well as the public for the BBS to have this disciplinary power. Making sure that the proverbial "bad apples" are prevented from continuing to work in the mental health professions increases public trust in those professionals who *do* follow the rules, and provides clients who have been harmed by their therapists an important avenue for justice.

How unprofessional conduct differs from ethical standards and from other laws

Ethical standards are developed by professional associations for a variety of purposes. These standards clarify the expectations of members of that profession, but can sometimes be unclear or even contradictory. Individuals who clearly violate the ethical standards of the profession can be censured by, or even kicked out of, their professional association. That action by itself may have little practical impact, however. You do not need to be an active member of your professional association to practice psychotherapy in California. It is the state, and not any professional association, that ultimately controls who can practice via licensure. So the state needs its own set of clear behavioral standards that it can enforce, in order to govern licensure appropriately. These behavioral standards are known collectively as unprofessional conduct statutes.

By defining an act in law as "unprofessional conduct," the state allows a licensing board to discipline the license of a person who engages in that act. For example, when Senate Bill 1172 prohibited therapists from performing "reparative therapy" with minors, it did this by defining reparative therapy (and therapies like it) as unprofessional conduct.[124]

A therapist who violates the law may be liable in three different contexts. A client may ask a court to award damages in a **civil** suit, where the client alleges that the therapist's actions were outside of the standards of the profession and caused them definable harm. Civil awards are typically money, and judges in these cases make decisions based on a *preponderance* (essentially, a majority) *of the evidence*. In a **criminal** case, the therapist is alleged to have violated the public in some way deserving of punishment. These cases can result in fines, jail time, or both. In order to be found guilty in a criminal trial, a judge or jury must find the evidence against you to be convincing *beyond a reasonable doubt*. A **disciplinary action** is focused on your performance in (or fitness for) a professional role, and the actions against you that can result are *based on that role*. Your license can be put on probation, suspended, or revoked, for example. You may be required to attend classes to refresh your knowledge about particular issues that led to the complaint against you. You may have to pay the costs of the BBS investigation, and may have fines levied against you. You will not, however, have to go to jail in a disciplinary action.

Since the potential consequences of a professional action are not as severe as those in a criminal case, the burden of proof is lower: The BBS uses a standard of "clear and convincing evidence," which is higher than the burden of proof in a civil case but lower than what is needed to convict someone of a criminal offense. There is more detail on the process of a disciplinary action, from complaint to resolution, later in this chapter.

It may be helpful to keep in mind that these three kinds of actions relate to different kinds of damage done, and they are not mutually exclusive. Egregious acts may lead to all three actions at once: If you commit insurance fraud, you are harming the insurance company (for which they may file a civil suit), violating a public standard (which can lead to criminal charges), *and* breaking the trust given to professionals (leading to possible action against your license).

---

[124] Senate Bill 1172 (Lieu), 2012. The law took effect in 2014 after it was challenged all the way to the United States Supreme Court. The Supreme Court refused to hear the case, allowing the law to take effect.

▶ Grounds for BBS action

> **The BBS can act against a license or registration for a variety of inappropriate acts.** Those acts are grouped into categories here.

The BBS lists 28 different types of violations that are considered unprofessional conduct under state law.[125] They are grouped into categories for easy reference here. Within each category you will find the specific violations as the BBS words them. In most cases, each of the three mental health professions covered in this text (LMFTs, LPCCs, and LCSWs) are bound by the same rules. The few exceptions to this are noted in their respective categories. Violation titles here generally are in the same wording as in the BBS *Disciplinary Guidelines.*[126]

Footnotes in this section refer to the places in law where the act listed is defined as unprofessional conduct. Information on penalties is drawn from the *Disciplinary Guidelines.* When penalties are discussed here, note that the focus is on the *minimum* penalty the BBS can impose for a particular offense. They will evaluate the severity of the case and the practitioner's history of similar acts in the past, and can impose harsher penalties based on these or other factors if they wish. In the most severe instances of almost all offenses, the practitioner's license or registration can be revoked. Also, there are several additional penalties that come with any violation of the unprofessional conduct statutes; we shall discuss these further when talking about the disciplinary process later in this chapter.

---

[125] Board of Behavioral Sciences (2013). *Disciplinary Guidelines.* Sacramento, CA: BBS. Downloadable here: www.bbs.ca.gov/pdf/publications/dispguid.pdf Note that the guidelines were updated as of July 1, 2013. New Disciplinary Guidelines will take effect during 2015, though the exact implementation date had not been determined at press time for this book.
[126] Board of Behavioral Sciences (2013). *Disciplinary Guidelines.* Sacramento, CA: BBS.

Sexual misconduct

Perhaps the area of professional misconduct that grabs the most attention is sexual misconduct. It certainly receives the harshest penalties – which makes some sense. Therapists are in a position of both power and emotional intimacy with clients, who often come to therapy in vulnerable states. For a therapist to engage in a sexual relationship with such a client can be very damaging to the client. It also undermines the public trust in *all* mental health professionals. It is considered such a violation of the professional relationship that **if a licensee or registrant is found to have had a sexual relationship with a client, or with a former client in the two years following the last professional contact, the BBS <u>must</u> revoke the license or registration.**[127] By law they cannot impose any lighter sentence. However, sex with a client is not the only form of sexual misconduct the BBS will take action on.

There are four different types of sexual misconduct, and one other related violation, spelled out in the unprofessional conduct statutes. *Sexual contact with client or former client* requires revocation of the license or registration, as noted above. *Engaging in an act with a minor punishable as a sexual offense, even if prior to registration or licensure,*[128] also typically results in a revoking of the license or registration. This keeps pedophiles out of the mental health professions. Note the careful language here – by using the language of an "act with a minor punishable as a sexual offense," this standard does not mean that the therapist must have actually been *convicted* of the sexual offense. So, if a therapist admits as part of a plea arrangement in a criminal case that they committed an act that could be punishable as a sexual offense, and in exchange prosecutors chose to use a lighter criminal charge, the BBS could still revoke the practitioner's license because of this language. *Commission of an act*

---

[127] California Business and Professions Code sections 4982.26, 4992.33, and 4999.90(k). The LPCC law does not require license revocation, but as a matter of practice, it appears likely that a license would be revoked in such circumstances.
[128] California Business and Professions Code sections 4982(aa)(1), 4992.3(x)(1), and 4999.90(z)(1)

punishable as a sexually related crime[129] uses similar language, applies regardless of whether the crime was before or after licensure, and similarly requires the BBS to revoke the license or registration. *Sexual misconduct*[130] is a lesser offense that covers any type of sexual misconduct except those that fall under the other types here. A therapist found to have violated this standard may have their license revoked, though not necessarily. Still, the penalties for a therapist engaging in any kind of sexual misconduct are harsh; for this last category, the minimum possible punishment includes a license suspension of at least 120 days, and 7 years of probation. The therapist also must retake, and pass, the licensing exams before they can resume practice.

As part of protecting the public from sexual misconduct by therapists, every member of the mental health professions is required to give the state-produced brochure "Professional Therapy Never Includes Sex"[131] to any client who says they have had a sexual relationship with a prior therapist. This helps the client to know that the previous therapist's actions were not appropriate, and gives the client guidance on how to report the previous therapist. *Failure to provide the sexual misconduct brochure*[132] is punishable with a minimum one-year probation.

The mental health professions have been getting gradually tougher on professionals who engage in sexual relationships with clients (current or former) or clients' family members. The 2014 ACA Code of Ethics has a five-year prohibition on sexual contact with former clients or their family members,[133] and the 2015 AAMFT Code of Ethics made it a lifetime prohibition.[134] The NASW Code, which does not offer a specific timeframe of prohibited sexual contact, makes it clear that such contact always poses significant risks.[135]

---

[129] California Business and Professions Code sections 4982(k), 4992.3(l), and 4999.90(k)
[130] California Business and Professions Code sections 4982(k), 4992.3(l), and 4999.90(k)
[131] California Department of Consumer Affairs: *Professional Therapy Never Includes Sex*. Sacramento, CA: DCA.
[132] California Business and Professions Code section 728
[133] ACA Code of Ethics, subprinciple A.5.c
[134] AAMFT Code of Ethics subprinciple 1.5
[135] NASW Code of Ethics subprinciple 1.09(c)

Although the legal standard here is shorter than the ethical standards, if you are successfully sued for sexual contact with a current or former client or a member of their family, your professional liability insurance will probably not cover you. Professional liability insurance policies routinely exclude sexual violations from coverage. They will provide for your defense in a trial, but if you admit or a court rules that you committed the act, your insurance will not pay any damages awarded to the plaintiff.[136]

Impairment

Therapists can lose their ability to practice effectively for a number of reasons. Just as we do not want drivers on the road whose driving is impaired by alcohol or other substances, we do not want therapists in practice whose behavior is so impaired as to be unsafe. ***Impaired ability to function safely due to mental illness, physical illness, or chemical dependency***[137] leads to a 60-day minimum suspension, which seems at least partly to be for the purpose of assessing whether the person will be able to continue in practice at all. Medical or psychological treatment may be required, and the therapist may see their practice restricted. In cases more directly impacting therapy, categorized as ***Chemical dependency or use of drugs with a client while performing services***,[138] at least a 120-day suspension is imposed, and the therapist must agree to abstain from substance use for the full term of their probation (at least 5 years) – including doing frequent blood or urine testing, which the therapist must pay for.

In keeping with state law, the BBS has voted to adopt new disciplinary guidelines that are especially tough on substance-related violations. These new regulations will take effect during 2015, though the exact implementation date had not been set as of press time for this book. For more on this, see Changes to Drug and Alcohol Rules later in this chapter.

---

[136] This is the policy of CPH and Associates, one of the larger professional liability insurance providers. Most liability insurers have similar rules.
[137] California Business and Professions Code sections 4982(c), 4982.1, 4992.3(c), 4992.35, and 4999.90(c)
[138] California Business and Professions Code sections 4982(c), 4982.1, 4992.3(c), 4992.35, and 4999.90(c)

Committing a crime or bad act

The BBS conducts background checks on all license and registration applicants to determine whether the applicant has a criminal history. Once a therapist is licensed or registered with the Board, the Board then automatically receives a report if the licensee or registrant is convicted of a crime in the future. The BBS can take action against anyone who has been convicted of a crime that is "substantially related to the qualifications, functions, or duties" of a therapist,[139] and they interpret that language broadly to mean any crime that shows "present or potential unfitness" of the person to perform therapy work in a manner consistent with public safety. *Conviction of a crime substantially related to the duties, functions, and responsibilities of a licensee or registrant* does not always lead to BBS action, however. Each case is evaluated individually. If you had a minor criminal conviction 15 years ago and have been out of trouble since, the BBS would of course examine the circumstances of your case, but it is unlikely they would discipline your license or registration (or prevent you from obtaining one). There are exceptions, of course, for crimes that fall into the sexual misconduct categories above. These acts *will* prevent someone from obtaining (or keeping) their license or registration. *Commission of a dishonest, corrupt, or fraudulent act substantially related to the duties, functions, and responsibilities of a licensee or registrant*[140] can result in enforcement actions against your license even if you are not convicted of a crime for that act. The minimum penalty for such an act includes 30 days suspension, 3 years of probation, and a Law and Ethics course.

---

[139] California Business and Professions Code sections 4982(a), 4992.3(a), and 4999.90(a); California Code of Regulations title 16 section 1812
[140] California Business and Professions Code sections 4982(j), 4992.3(k), and 4999.90(j)

Fraud and misrepresentation

Anyone found to be responsible for *Securing (or attempting to secure) a license by fraud*[141] – the most common example being lying to the BBS on your license or registration application – automatically has that license or registration revoked.

There are two basic ways that you can misrepresent yourself in the therapy world. You can misrepresent your own licensure status, or you can pretend to be someone else who is licensed.

Misrepresentation of (your own) license or qualifications[142] leads to a minimum 60-day suspension, 3 years minimum probation, and possibly having to retake licensing exams. This kind of punishment would be given to an MFT intern who advertised as being fully licensed, for example. This can happen outside of marketing contexts as well – an LPCC intern who claimed to be licensed while billing insurance for a client's therapy would also be committing this offense (and others).

Impersonating a licensee[143] is the other kind of misrepresentation. It occurs when someone who is not licensed tells a client or others that they are actually someone else, when that someone else *is* licensed. This, too, can occur in the context of insurance billing, if an intern or associate attempts to bill an insurance company by suggesting that it was actually their supervisor who provided the therapy being charged. A supervisor who supports such behavior is also committing this offense, as the language includes *allowing* impersonation. This violation is met with a minimum 60-day suspension and 5-year probation.

---

[141] California Business and Professions Code sections 4982(a), 4992.3(a), and 4999.90(a)

[142] California Business and Professions Code sections 4982(f), 4992.3(g), and 4999.90(f)

[143] California Business and Professions Code sections 4982(g), 4992.3(h), and 4999.90(g)

Assisting someone practicing without a license

If someone is practicing in California without a license, then by definition, there is no license for the BBS to act against. (The state could pursue a *criminal* case against that person, since practicing without a license is a crime.) However, if a licensed or registered person helped in the unlicensed activity, then the BBS would discipline that person for *Aiding and abetting unlicensed activity.*[144] For example, a licensee who described their colleague as being licensed when making referrals to the colleague, knowing that the colleague was not actually licensed, would be aiding unlicensed activity. This is punished with a minimum 30-day suspension and 3 years of probation. This charge could also be applied to *unregistered* activity; a supervisor who allowed a recent graduate to work in their private practice before registering with the BBS could be considered to be aiding unregistered activity. (Recall that registration is needed before working in a private practice.)

Testing-related violations

It is essential to the fairness and validity of any testing process that those who take the test are who they say they are, do not attempt to cheat on the test, and do not reveal any information about test content to those who have not yet taken the exam. This is certainly true with licensing exams, which are considered high-stakes tests because failing directly impact's one's professional standing and job opportunities. *Violating exam security or subverting a license exam*[145] occurs most commonly when someone who has just taken their exam shares its content with others who have not yet taken the exam. This is punished with a minimum of 5 years probation and retaking of classes. "Subverting," as it is used here, means impacting the integrity of the exam; while sharing content is perhaps the most common way this happens, it certainly is not the only way it could

---

[144] California Business and Professions Code sections 4982(h), 4992.3(i), and 4999.90(h)
[145] California Business and Professions Code sections 4982(ab), 4992.3(z), and 4999.90(aa)

occur. Someone who hacks into the testing centers' computer network to give examinees extra time is also subverting the exam process.

It is worth mentioning here that violating exam security is not always an obvious thing. Of course it would be a violation to use your phone's camera to take pictures of exam questions, and then to share them with others about to take the test. That is one of many reasons why testing centers do not allow phones. But violating exam security can also happen in subtler ways.

In recent years, a number of social media groups have sprung up to help provide social support to those in various stages of their careers, including some groups specifically focused on prelicensed therapists. In those groups, people who have recently taken their licensing exams can provide very helpful social and emotional support to those who are about to test. However, I have seen several instances of group members posting questions like "What will I need to know about cognitive-behavioral interventions for my exam?"

When someone who has recently taken a licensing exam answers that question, they likely have good intentions; they're trying to help a fellow professional to focus their preparation on those pieces that will be most helpful. But in doing that, they are giving the person who asked for the information an unfair advantage in testing. Licensing exams are only fair if everyone goes into them on a level playing field in terms of their awareness of specific exam content. If you are a member of such groups on any social media site, and you see specific discussion of exam content, please do all you can to prevent test information from being posted or shared. Obviously there is risk to those who are sharing test information, as they could lose their (sometimes brand new) license over it. But there is also significant risk for all those anxiously preparing for their own upcoming exams, whether members of the particular group or not: If the BBS learns that exam content is being circulated among those who have not yet tested, one possible response would be for them to simply shut down that cycle of the exam, and not allow *anyone* to test until the next exam cycle starts in six months with new exam content.

While it is not broken into a distinct category in the BBS Disciplinary Guidelines, the law also defines public disclosure of psychological tests as unprofessional conduct when the validity of the test depends upon the public being unfamiliar with it. Personality tests, such as the MMPI or the Rorschach, are among those tests that cannot be shared publicly. "Disclosure" here does not only mean sharing the test itself – even *describing* the test publicly in detail could be considered a violation.[146]

Discipline by another state or board

While it is not common, some therapists maintain more than one professional license. Some, especially those who live close to state lines, may have licenses in multiple states. Others may have two licenses within the same state, such as a therapist who licenses as an LPCC after the completion of a master's degree and chooses to maintain an LPCC license even after completing a doctoral degree and getting licensed as a Psychologist. If the BBS learns that another state or government agency has acted against your license or registration with that other agency, of course it makes sense that the BBS would want to investigate the circumstances of that discipline. If it reflects poorly on your ability to work safely within your BBS license, then *Discipline by another state or governmental agency*[147] will also lead to discipline from the BBS. Of course, they will review the relevant laws; if you were disciplined in another state for an act that is legally acceptable in California, the BBS may choose not to take any action.

Failure to maintain confidentiality

At first glance, this may appear to be an easy problem to avoid: Keeping records secure and not revealing what clients have told you in therapy are clear standards. However, many violations of confidentiality occur accidentally. A therapist slips up and uses the actual name of their client in a public discussion. Cars and computers get stolen with client records inside. Or, as happened to a therapist in the United Kingdom, clients recognize themselves as the subjects of social media discussion even when the therapist never uses specific names.[148] *Failure to maintain confidentiality*[149] is met with a

---

[146] California Business and Professions Code sections 4982(q), 4992.3(r), and 4999.90(q)

[147] California Business and Professions Code sections 4982.25, 4992.36, and 4990.38

[148] www.dailymail.co.uk/news/article-2755853/

minimum 60-day suspension and 3 years probation, required educational classes and retaking of licensure exams.

Supervision-related violations

Supervisors of trainees, interns, and associates are responsible for the conduct of those under their supervision. While the common phrasing of working "under the supervisor's license" is technically inaccurate – a trainee, intern, or associate is working under their *supervision*, not their license – a supervisor can be held responsible in addition to the supervisee if the supervisee commits acts of misconduct, or if the supervisor does not live up to the supervisor's legal obligations.

There are two types of unprofessional misconduct in this category. *Improper supervision of a trainee, intern, associate, or supervisee*[150] occurs when a supervisor is failing to abide by the legal responsibility for oversight of the supervisee's work. This includes monitoring the supervisee's cases and records. It is punishable by a minimum of 30 days suspension and 2 years probation. Of course, "improper" is a somewhat vague word. Some codes of ethics provide more detail than the law does about the specific expectations of supervisors. This is important, as the BBS will often review professional ethical codes to determine whether a supervisor has failed to live up to their profession's standard of care for supervision. If it is the supervisee, instead of the supervisor, who commits an unprofessional act, but the supervisor knew or reasonably should have known about the violation, this would likely fall under *Violations of the chapter or regulations by licensees or registrants / Violations involving acquisition and supervision of required hours of experience.*[151] These violations are punishable by a minimum one-year probation. Any hours of experience gained illegally are automatically revoked.

---

[149] California Business and Professions Code sections 4982(m), 4992.3(n), and 4999.90(m)
[150] California Business and Professions Code sections 4982(r), 4992.3(s), and 4999.90(r)
[151] California Business and Professions Code sections 4982(e) and (u), 4992.3(f), and 4999.90(e) and (u)

Fees and advertising

In Chapter 4, we will learn about the state requirements for what must be disclosed to clients before therapy begins. This includes a requirement to disclose what fee the client is being charged and how that fee was computed. *Failure to disclose fees in advance*[152] is a serious offense, but certainly not as serious as sexual misconduct or some of the other acts described here. For this reason, it is one of the few acts of unprofessional conduct where the maximum penalty is not revoking the license. The minimum penalty for failing to disclose fees is one year of probation; the *maximum* penalty includes a 30-day suspension and 2 years probation.

In Chapter 8, we will see that the state's laws surrounding how therapists market themselves are quite specific. *False, misleading, deceptive, or improper advertising*[153] leads to a minimum one-year probation. As with failing to disclose fees, this is not considered as severe an offense as many others; the maximum penalty here includes a 60-day suspension and 5 years probation, but does not allow for a license to be revoked.

Finally, if you refer a client to another health care professional, this should be an unbiased act, made solely based on the best interests of the client. For this reason, *Paying, accepting, or soliciting a fee for referrals* is met with a minimum of 3 years probation and a required course in law and ethics.[154]

Record-keeping

It seems basic that therapists would need to keep records on the services they have provided to clients. Under a new law that took effect January 1, 2015, LMFTs, LPCCs, and LCSWs all must retain client records for at least seven years after the end of therapy. If the client is

---

[152] California Business and Professions Code sections 4982(n), 4992.3(o), and 4999.90(n)
[153] California Business and Professions Code sections 651, 4982(p), 4992.3(q), and 4999.90(p)
[154] California Business and Professions Code sections 4982(o), 4992.3(p), and 4999.90(o)

a minor, their records must be retained until the client's 25th birthday (that is, seven years after they turn 18).[155]

Surprisingly, surveys of therapists show a small percentage who refuse to keep any records at all.[156] *Failure to keep records consistent with sound clinical judgment*[157] leads to at least a year of probation. It seems likely that violations of the new seven-year standard for retaining records would be disciplined under this category.

As we will see in Chapter 5 on Confidentiality, clients have a right to access their records (with some meaningful exceptions) – one of many reasons it is expected that you will have records in the first place. *Willful failure to comply with clients' requests for access to mental health records*[158] also leads to at least a year of probation.

The maximum penalties for violating these standards are not as harsh as those for some of the other standards. Maximum penalties in each of these areas include 30 days of suspension and 3 years of probation.

Practicing beyond license or competence

As we saw in the previous chapter, the titles of "Licensed Marriage and Family Therapist," "Licensed Clinical Social Worker," and "Licensed Professional Clinical Counselor" are meaningful. Each one comes with specific requirements and limitations, and each license takes a lot of time and work to earn. It is important that the practice of psychotherapy be limited to those appropriately qualified to do it. Even within the professions, it is important that you be trained specifically to deliver the services you provide. It is not professional to try out a new type of therapy you do not know well on an unsuspecting client who has placed their trust in you to provide good care. *Performing, offering, or representing yourself as able*

---

[155] Senate Bill 578 (Wyland), 2014.
[156] Surveys done by CAMFT and others over the past several years typically show about 3-5% of respondents saying they do not keep any records at all.
[157] California Business and Professions Code sections 4982(v), 4992.3(t), and 4999.90(v)
[158] California Business and Professions Code sections 4982(y), 4992.3(w), and 4999.90(ad)

to perform a service outside of your scope of practice or competence[159] is a serious offense punishable with a minimum 30-day suspension and 3 years of probation. A supervisor who allows their supervisee to do such a thing is also considered to have committed this offense.

Telemedicine violations

In Chapter 9 (Technology), we will discuss the California Telemedicine Act, which sets standards for therapists and other healthcare providers who offer services via phone, Internet, or other technology. *Violating the state telehealth standards*[160] (most commonly, by failing to obtain or record client consent for telehealth services) results in a minimum of one year of probation and required educational coursework.

General misconduct, negligence, recklessness, or willful harm

The categories reviewed so far will not capture every inappropriate professional act. So the BBS also has at its disposal additional categories that are less specific. These serve to prevent licensees or registrants from avoiding discipline based on technicalities or arguments about the meaning of a particular word. They also can be useful when the BBS is engaging in what is essentially plea bargaining with a licensee under investigation; we will tackle that process in the next section.

General unprofessional conduct[161] and *gross negligence or incompetence*[162] are catch-all categories for behavior that is well

---

[159] California Business and Professions Code sections 4982(l), (s), and (t); 4992.3(m); and 4999.90(l), (s), and (t); California Code of Regulations title 16 sections 1881(g) and (h)

[160] California Business and Professions Code sections 4982(z), 4992.3(x); 4999.90(ac); and 2290.5(b) and (c)

[161] California Business and Professions Code sections 4982, 4992.3, and 4999.90

[162] California Business and Professions Code sections 4982(d), 4992.3(d) and (e), and 4999.90(d)

outside of professional standards but does not readily fit into the more specific categories listed above.

One example of general unprofessional conduct would be failing to file a mandated report of child, elder, or dependent adult abuse. Under California law, mental health professionals are required to report such abuse (more on these reporting requirements can be found in Chapters 6 and 7). The mandated reporting laws come with specific timeframes, which changed significantly for elder and dependent adult abuse in 2012.[163] Failing to file a mandated report is problematic for multiple reasons, the most troubling of which is that it potentially allows an abuser to continue to abuse the same or other victims.

Another example of general unprofessional conduct is to offer so-called reparative therapy, also known as conversion therapy or ex-gay therapy, to minors. Under a law passed in 2012 that took effect in 2014 (see Chapter 10 for more on the story of this bill), any mental health professional is committing unprofessional conduct if they attempt to change the sexual orientation of a minor through therapy.[164]

A third example of unprofessional conduct comes when you are under investigation for another possible violation. Under regulations that took effect in 2013, it can be considered unprofessional conduct to refuse to participate in, or cooperate with, a BBS investigation. It is also now considered unprofessional conduct to refuse to turn over records to the BBS within 15 days of their request when they are conducting an investigation.[165] While there are some exceptions in these rules to protect therapists, it is noteworthy that either of these charges can result in action against your license or registration even if the original complaint that sparked the investigation turns out to be groundless.

General unprofessional conduct is punished with a minimum 60-day suspension and 3 years of probation; gross negligence or incompetence is punished with a minimum 60-day suspension, 5 years of probation, and having to retake the licensing exams.

---

[163] See Chapter 7, Working with Elders and Dependent Adults
[164] California Business and Professions Code section 865
[165] California Code of Regulations title 16 sections 1823, 1845, 1858, and 1881

Intentionally or recklessly causing physical or emotional harm to a client[166] occurs when a therapist not only has violated the standards of their profession, but has done so in a such a way that a client has truly suffered as a result. This is considered a severe violation, and so even the minimum penalty is severe: 90 days of suspension, 5 years of probation, and retaking licensing exams will all be required.

Violations of the chapter or regulations by licensees or registrants / Violations involving acquisition and supervision of required hours of experience[167] was mentioned above, in discussing supervision-related violations. This category (particularly its first half) also addresses in general terms any violations of the licensing acts of each of the professions covered in this text. These violations are punishable by a minimum one-year probation. Any hours of experience gained illegally are automatically revoked.

---

[166] California Business and Professions Code sections 4982(i), 4992.3(j), and 4999.90(i)

[167] California Business and Professions Code sections 4982(e) and (u), 4992.3(f), and 4999.90(e) and (u)

▶ The disciplinary process

> **Most actions against a license or registration are initiated by either a consumer complaint or a law enforcement report of a therapist's arrest or criminal conviction.** The process is designed to give the professional a fair hearing, but it is not like a civil or criminal trial.

For the six-month span of April through September 2014, the BBS received 673 consumer complaints against its licensees and registrants.[168] At first that number may sound high, but it is actually fairly low when you consider that there are more than 75,000 licensed and registered mental health professionals under BBS jurisdiction in California.[169] Consider as well that a majority of complaints are closed without the need for a field investigation or hearing. The number of therapists who commit an act so outside of accepted professional standards as to warrant action against their license or registration is actually quite low.

One way to look at this is through raw frequency numbers; in the first quarter of the 2014-15 fiscal year there were a total of 588 issues presented to the BBS (291 consumer complaints plus 297 arrest or conviction reports of licensees and registrants), and in that same time, just 27 final disciplinary orders were adopted.[170] Another way to look at this is through the lens of how much it costs you to purchase professional liability insurance; mental health professionals actually pay less than many other health care professionals, because of both a lower frequency of complaints and lower monetary awards when

---

[168] Materials for the August 27-28, 2014 meeting of the Board of Behavioral Sciences, page 15, and supplemental materials for the November 19-20, 2014 meeting of the Board of Behavioral Sciences, page 19

[169] Board of Behavioral Sciences: Licensee and Registrant Statistics

[170] Supplemental materials for the November 19-20, 2014 meeting of the Board of Behavioral Sciences, pages 19-20. This is not a perfect apples-to-apples set of data, since most of the cases closed would have originated in earlier months. However, the numbers of licensees and registrants disciplined in any given year is similarly low compared to the total population of professionals.

lawsuits are either won by complainants or settled before going to trial.

Few therapists ever want to be the subject of a complaint. But if you *are* ever the subject of an investigation, or if a client wants your help as they prepare to file a complaint against a previous therapist, it will help you to know how the process works. It can be roughly broken down into four stages: Complaint, Investigation, Hearing, and Resolution. The BBS web site describes the entire process, from complaint to resolution, as taking about two years,[171] though their own data suggests that it often takes longer.[172]

Complaint

The BBS accepts complaints against licensees or registrants through its web site or via mail. While complaints may be made anonymously, doing so sometimes makes it more difficult for the BBS to conduct a proper investigation. For example, an anonymous complaint about a therapist's advertisement can still be investigated; the BBS would be interested in the content of the ad, not the identity of the complainant. But if an anonymous complaint is received about something that took place in a therapy session, the BBS cannot go on a proverbial "fishing expedition" through a therapist's records without knowing which client was potentially harmed.

When the BBS first receives a complaint, it is reviewed by their staff to determine whether it is against a person who is actually licensed or registered with the BBS. If not, there is no license or registration to discipline; the BBS might keep the complaint on file in case the subject of the complaint ever applies for a license or registration in the future, and it might forward the complaint to another enforcement agency if appropriate. If the subject of the complaint *is* a licensee or registrant, then the complaint is evaluated based on whether it would be actionable *if everything in the complaint were true*. A client complaint about the color of paint on your walls will not be pursued. Perhaps more to the point, a client complaint about therapy that was simply ineffective will not be pursued, so long

---

[171] Board of Behavioral Sciences: *Complaint Process*
[172] Supplemental materials for the November 19-20, 2014 meeting of the Board of Behavioral Sciences, page 20

as the therapist's actions were within all legal and ethical boundaries and in keeping with the standard of care for the profession. Therapy does not always work, and a therapeutic failure in and of itself is not a reason for a therapist to be disciplined. If the complaint is against a current licensee or registrant, *and* is something that would be actionable if true, it is forwarded to the BBS's investigative unit.

Investigation

Investigations can take a very long time. Again, it takes more than two years from the time a complaint is received for a disciplinary order to be finalized, in an average case. Some take months or even years longer. Most cases are investigated by the Division of Investigation, though allegations of misconduct that would also be criminal offenses may be investigated through other agencies. Partly because the DOI investigators have such heavy caseloads, it may be months between a complaint being filed and that same complaint being actively investigated. The investigation often involves interviews with the person filing the complaint and the therapist accused of wrongdoing, as well as others relevant to the issue. Depending on the nature of the complaint, it may also involve a review of the therapist's records for the case being investigated. Other records may be brought in as needed, such as the therapist's educational transcripts.

During the time a complaint is being investigated, therapists typically can go on practicing as usual. Not all investigations lead to discipline, of course, and a therapist should not be restricted from practice while a complaint is being investigated in case it turns out that the complaint is groundless. Exceptions are made in the case of therapists who may present an immediate danger to their clients; for example, a therapist who is in the throes of a substance abuse problem may be immediately suspended from practicing while an investigation is ongoing.

Therapists are required to cooperate with the investigation process and to produce records when requested, as noted earlier in this chapter. However, the investigator should not be viewed as a friend to the therapist. The investigator's role is to determine the facts of the case so that the BBS can decide whether the therapist poses a danger to the public requiring disciplinary action against the therapist's license.

Therapists accused of wrongdoing often bring in a lawyer early in the investigation process. Legal counsel, typically provided for the therapist by their professional liability insurer, can help ensure that the therapist is cooperating with the investigation while also protecting the therapist's own interests.

Many cases are not pursued past the investigation stage. If the investigation confirms the allegations in the original complaint, the BBS may forward the case to the office of the Attorney General to begin formal disciplinary action. A formal Accusation is then filed against the therapist, who has the right to request a hearing to fight the charges.[173]

Before a hearing is held, the BBS will often work with those formally accused of misconduct to see whether they can reach a settlement, or a **stipulation**. In a stipulation, the therapist accused of unprofessional conduct admits to certain specific violations and agrees that a particular set of disciplinary actions can be imposed.[174] If you are familiar with the process of plea bargaining in criminal cases (fans of TV crime shows like *Law & Order* will know this process well), the process of reaching a stipulation can be similar, if less dramatic. The state may agree to pursue a lesser punishment if the accused person simply admits that the alleged act took place rather than continuing to fight the charges. When a case is settled through stipulation, there is no formal hearing. The case skips ahead to the resolution phase.

Hearing

Disciplinary hearings take place in the presence of an Administrative Law Judge. In some ways these hearings look like criminal trials, with the state and the accused person each presenting their case and calling witnesses. However, recall from the beginning of this chapter that a disciplinary hearing does not require a therapist to be proven guilty beyond a reasonable doubt. The burden of proof here is *clear and convincing evidence*, which is something of a lower bar. The Administrative Law Judge weighs the facts as presented, and writes a *proposed* decision on the matter. This judge does not have the

---

[173] Board of Behavioral Sciences: *Complaint Process*
[174] Board of Behavioral Sciences: *Complaint Process*

final say, however. The judge's proposed decision is forwarded to the BBS for their consideration.

Resolution

The BBS – and here, I refer simply to the 13 members who actually make up the Board,[175] not the full staff of the organization – can choose to adopt or not adopt any proposed decision in a disciplinary action. This applies to both Administrative Law Judge proposed decisions that result from hearings, and stipulations that result from negotiations between an accused therapist and the state. In most cases, the BBS will accept the proposed decision or stipulation. In some cases, they review the case and instead issue a different decision or different discipline. Either way, the therapist can appeal for reconsideration of the case or appeal through the state court system.[176]

If a licensee or registrant is disciplined, the suspension and probation periods noted above are not the only elements of the therapist's punishment. Standard terms and conditions include cost recovery (that is, the therapist must pay for the costs of the BBS investigation of them), notifying all employers and clients of the disciplinary action, and filing quarterly reports with the BBS regarding probation compliance. Licensees or registrants on probation also cannot supervise any interns, associates, or trainees, and cannot serve as instructors for continuing education. Those on probation also must maintain their license or registration, and commit to obeying all laws.[177]

The BBS also has several additional optional requirements that they may choose to impose as part of a disciplinary order. These include requiring the therapist to retake licensing exams, take a law and ethics course, hire an outside monitor or auditor for their billing system (common when the discipline is for billing-related issues), undergo psychological or psychiatric examinations, participate in psychotherapy, have their practice supervised or otherwise restricted, and pay the costs of their own probation. Any therapist disciplined for issues surrounding drug and alcohol use will also be required to

---

[175] California Business and Professions Code section 4990(a)
[176] Board of Behavioral Sciences: *Complaint Process*
[177] Board of Behavioral Sciences: *Disciplinary Guidelines*

abstain from substance use and submit to regular testing – at the therapist's expense – to verify that they are not using.[178]

As you can see, any disciplinary action has a major impact on a therapist's practice. Thankfully, avoiding such actions is not simply a matter of hoping for the best. There are many proactive steps a therapist can take to protect their practices.

---

[178] Board of Behavioral Sciences: *Disciplinary Guidelines*. See Changes to drug and alcohol rules (next page) for additional information.

▶ Changes to drug and alcohol rules

> **Strict new rules for drug and alcohol-related violations will take effect during 2015.**

A state law passed in 2008 created a task force to develop recommendations for how the state could better deal with those who had licenses from the state (in a wide variety of health care professions) but were abusing drugs or alcohol.[179] Based on the task force recommendations, the Department of Consumer Affairs, which oversees the BBS, developed final rules each of its boards and bureaus needed to follow. Those rules are called the *Uniform Standards Related to Substance Abuse*, or more simply known just as the Uniform Standards.[180] The Uniform Standards are intended to protect consumers from potentially dangerous professionals. As you will see, the penalties required by the Uniform Standards can be tough. The BBS has very little leeway to deviate from them.

At some point during 2015, the Uniform Standards will become a part of the BBS's Disciplinary Guidelines.[181] Because the Uniform Standards must be formally adopted through regulation, their exact implementation date was not known at press time for this book, though April 1 and July 1 were seen as the most likely possibilities.

Under the new rules, certain penalties will be automatic with all substance abuse violations. Other penalties, if applied, cannot be reduced based on specific circumstances of the case. The punishments for substance-related violations will include:

- **A clinical diagnostic evaluation** to determine whether the therapist has a substance use disorder. Notably, even if this evaluation results in a finding that the licensee or registrant

---

[179] Senate Bill 1441 (Ridley-Thomas), 2008

[180] Department of Consumer Affairs (2011). *Uniform standards regarding substance-abusing healing arts licensees.* Sacramento, CA: DCA.

[181] The remaining information in this section all comes from the BBS-approved regulations that are, at press time, awaiting final approval from the state. They can be read here: www.bbs.ca.gov/pdf/regulation/2014/sb1441_mod_language.pdf

does *not* have a diagnosable substance use problem, other penalties are likely to remain in effect.

- **Mandatory drug and alcohol testing** to ensure the therapist is not continuing to use substances. No licensee or registrant put on probation for a substance use violation will be allowed to return to practice until they have at least 30 days of negative drug tests. For the first year of probation, the therapist will be randomly drug tested between 52 and 104 times each year; they must make *daily* contact with a testing center to see whether they have been randomly selected to test that day. In years 2-5, testing is reduced to between 36 and 104 times per year. Any planned vacations or absences must be pre-approved by the BBS, who will approve alternative drug testing locations close to where the therapist will be. Failure to report for required testing, or testing positive for alcohol or any controlled substance, will be punished with *automatic and immediate* suspension of the license or registration and referral back to the BBS for additional disciplinary action. The therapist's employer will be immediately notified of the suspension.

- In addition to the above, the BBS can mandate supervised practice, restricted practice, participation in chemical dependency support or recovery group meetings, and other standard terms and conditions of probation. Perhaps most significantly, those who are on probation are typically required to pay for the costs of the investigation into their violation and the costs of probation. As you can imagine, the costs of drug testing alone – up to 520 tests over five years of probation – can easily reach tens of thousands of dollars for those therapists who commit substance use violations.

▶ Protecting yourself

> **There are a few common-sense practices that can help reduce risks to your practice.** Most importantly, know the rules of your profession and practice within them.

The purpose of this chapter is not to make you fear for your license. It is to make you familiar with the disciplinary rules and the disciplinary process, so that you are best aware of the rules that apply in the state of California. Both the standards themselves and the disciplinary process may vary in other states. Following California's standards is not a guarantee that you will avoid ever having a complaint or lawsuit filed against you, but it *can* help prevent that complaint or lawsuit from damaging or even ending your career. This section focuses on five common-sense things you can do that will help ensure that your practice is as safe as possible.

A reminder here is in order: **I am not a lawyer, so please do not interpret any of this as legal advice.** I am a therapist, and so this is intended as common-sense advice on running a sound and clinically-appropriate therapy practice. If you are interested in more specific advice on risk management and risk avoidance from a legal perspective, I would strongly encourage you to consult with a lawyer. In many cases, you can obtain qualified legal advice for free through your professional liability insurance or your professional association membership.

1. Maintain familiarity with professional standards

California's state laws for mental health professionals change every year, often significantly. It is vital to remember that laws are not set in stone. They are living documents, meant to adapt to changing social conditions, and any changes to the law do impact you. You cannot simply carry on in your career presuming that your profession's rules are still the ones that were in effect when you initially went to graduate school, or when you first obtained your license.

It is for this reason that California requires licensees to take a six-hour continuing education course in Law and Ethics in each two-year license renewal period. Ideally, this keeps practitioners up to date with the great many changes in state law and ethical standards that can occur, even in a short timeframe. In addition, membership in professional associations (listed at the end of this chapter) and attendance at their conferences and events can help you stay in the loop on changes in law or policy that directly impact your work.

It is worth noting here that if you are a supervisor, you have specific additional obligations to your supervisees to remain current in your understanding of state law and professional ethical standards, and to supervise accordingly. Directing a supervisee to work in a manner that is inconsistent with current state law could be considered "improper supervision," one of the types of unprofessional conduct detailed above.[182]

2. Maintain professional liability insurance

This may be the single most important purchase you make as a professional. For a relatively low price – some professional associations will even give student members professional liability insurance for free – you can have easy access to attorneys and protection from complaints or lawsuits against you. You may go through your entire career never *needing* your liability insurance, but it will provide a great deal of peace of mind to know that you have it just in case.

Professional liability insurers offer multiple types of protection. Most commonly, they will insure you against claims made against you for actions taken in your professional role, so long as those actions were not intentionally harmful. Depending on your insurance company and the type of policy you choose, you may also get general liability insurance (sometimes called "slip-and-fall" coverage) and coverage for the costs of defending you during a licensing board investigation.

As mentioned earlier, policies make exclusions for sexual acts with clients, since those are presumed to be intentional. But if a client sues you or complains about you because they did not like the outcome of your work, and you have acted responsibly and professionally, your liability insurance can feel like a lifesaver.

---

[182] California Business and Professions Code sections 4982(r), 4992.3(s), and 4999.90(r)

3. Address potential complaints

     If you have clients who you know are unhappy with the service they have received from you – or if, in an even worse situation, you become aware that you have accidentally committed a violation of the unprofessional conduct statutes – potential complaints can sometimes be addressed informally and resolved to the client's satisfaction. Of course, you should not try to use force to prevent someone from filing a complaint against you, and it is against the law to include a "no-licensure-complaint" clause in a settlement agreement that avoids or ends a civil lawsuit.[183] But working with clients to minimize any harm they might experience because of inadvertent violations is consistent with the mental health professions' ethical values of beneficence and nonmalfeasance, and may convince a dissatisfied client that a formal complaint is not needed. Research in the field of medicine shows that when doctors apologize and take responsibility for medical mistakes, rather than taking a defensive posture, their patients are more satisfied and less likely to sue.[184]

4. Keep excellent records

     As detailed above, keeping records consistent with sound clinical judgment is a requirement for licensed mental health professionals. Such records also can be especially useful in defending yourself from an accusation of improper conduct.

     If a client makes a claim that an intervention from your session on November 16 harmed them and was not professional practice, simply telling the BBS, "No, I did not do that!" is not likely to be considered a full or adequate defense. You are likely to be much better off if you have thorough records from that day's session that detail what interventions you did use and how the client responded to them. It also can be helpful if records from sessions after that day showed the client's continued engagement in therapy without any noticeable worsening of symptoms. In any situation where it is a client's word against that of the therapist, naturally one of the first places the BBS

---

[183] California Business and Professions Code section 143.5
[184] Robbennolt, J. K. (2009). Apologies and medical error. *Clinical Orthopaedics and Related Research, 467*(2), 376-382.

would look for additional information is in the therapist's documentation. If a client claims that they experienced harm as a result of the therapy, can they document that harm? Or instead, can you show that your actions in therapy were well within accepted professional standards?

5. Follow the law, even in non-professional contexts

You may have noticed at the beginning of this section that the BBS receives arrest and conviction reports on its licensees and registrants. It receives roughly as many of these as consumer complaints. While consumer complaints necessarily involve your professional conduct, arrest and conviction reports go to the BBS regardless of whether the crime you were charged with had anything to do with your professional role.

As described earlier in this chapter, conviction of a crime related to the duties, functions, and responsibilities of a therapist is cause for disciplinary action. There are also several acts that do not require criminal convictions in order for the BBS to act against your license, if the arrest report suggests that you may not be able to function safely in your professional role. Recall as well that the BBS takes a broad view of what may reflect on your fitness for your professional role, and you can see that your responsibility to abide by a higher standard of behavior than the average person does not only apply while you are in the office.

Among the most common offenses the BBS disciplines its licensees and registrants for are substance use offenses, particularly driving under the influence of alcohol or other drugs (DUI). The impact of a DUI conviction will last for years on your professional life as well as your personal life. As you have read, the penalties taking effect in 2015 for substance use violations can be quite severe.

Simply put, one of the best things you can do to protect your practice is to take a cab if you've been drinking.

4

Informed Consent

It is a fundamental principle in health care that clients have the right to know what specific treatments are being performed on them. This way they can make active and informed choices as to whether they want each treatment. California law includes some specific requirements for information clients need prior to the beginning of therapy. Additional requirements come from professional ethics codes and each profession's standard of care.

▶ The underlying principle

It is a longstanding principle across the healthcare professions that patients should know what they are getting into with any medical treatment, so they can make an active choice whether to receive that treatment. While state law does not provide much guidance for what needs to be included in an informed consent agreement, a therapist who fails to engage their client in an informed consent process can have their license disciplined for unprofessional conduct (see Chapter 3, Unprofessional Conduct).

In basic terms, an informed consent process involves describing for your client what treatments will be performed and for what purposes. Clients are also informed of the "ground rules" for therapy, including confidentiality and its exceptions (see Chapter 5, Confidentiality, Privilege, and Exceptions). Informed consent also includes information about fees and billing practices, as we will see below.

Ultimately, the larger idea of informed consent is every bit as important as the more specific requirements. Every professional ethics code in mental health emphasizes the importance of client autonomy and **self-determination**, the right of clients to choose for themselves what treatment to take part in and what goals to pursue in therapy. The more information a client has about the therapy process before it begins, the better position they are in to act from a place of autonomy and self-determination.

In this chapter, we discuss primarily the state requirements for informed consent. It is important to understand, however, that your ethical code is likely to describe specific required elements of informed consent in more detail, and you are obligated to the specific requirements of your ethical code as well as state law.

▶ California's disclosure requirements

In *Cobbs v. Grant*, the California court case that defined health care providers' informed consent obligations, four principles of informed consent were outlined:[185]

1. Clients do not usually have the same expert knowledge as health care providers.
2. A client has the right to control their participation in treatment, including the right to choose whether to participate in treatment.
3. A client needs information, particularly about the benefits and risks of treatment, to make an effective decision about whether to participate in treatment.
4. A client relies on the health care provider to give them that information in terms the client can understand.

However, state law offers little in the way of more direct guidance on what an informed consent agreement should include. State law specifies surprisingly few things that a client must be informed of prior to mental health care; those requirements are described below. However, the standard of care for such agreements within your profession may include additional information, which we will cover in the next section.

Any disclosures made to the client as part of an informed consent process should be in easily understood language. Informed consent documents or conversations that are in language too complex or sophisticated for clients to understand do little good in actually informing them.

---

[185] *Cobbs v. Grant*, 8 Cal. 3d 229 (1972)

Fees

The state requires that clients be informed, prior to the beginning of mental health treatment, of what the fee will be. Clients also must be informed about how the fee was computed.[186] For example, is yours a standard fee charged to all clients for each hour of service? Or is it set on a sliding fee scale, based on the client's income? Either of these is allowed, of course. The client simply must know before treatment begins how much they will be paying for it and why the fee is what it is.

Licensure status

All licensees and registrants are required to post their licenses or registrations in a clearly visible place in their offices.[187] This helps ensure that clients will be aware of the licensure of their therapist before treatment. The law is a not clear as to whether this information actually needs to be part of informed consent, but given the disclosure requirements for all therapist advertising (see Chapter 8, Advertising), it seems like good sense to ensure in any informed consent agreement that clients are at least made aware of your license or registration title and number.

If a therapist is operating a private practice under a fictitious business name (for example, if I called my practice the "Anytown Counseling Center"), the client must be informed of who actually owns the business, and what their licensure status is.[188]

Any trainee, intern, or associate providing therapy must inform the client, prior to the beginning of treatment, of their licensure status and that they are under licensed supervision. They also must provide the name of their employer.[189]

---

[186] California Business and Professions Code sections 4982(n), 4992.3(o), and 4999.90(n)
[187] California Business and Professions Code sections 4980.31, 4996.7, and 4999.70
[188] California Business and Professions Code sections 4980.46, 4992.10, and 4999.72
[189] California Business and Professions Code sections 4980.44(c), 4980.48(a), 4996.18(h), 4999.36(d), and 4999.45(a)(3)

Technology

If you will be using technology as part of the delivery of services, California law requires that you obtain and document the client's verbal consent for telehealth services. This applies to therapy by videoconference, telephone, or any other technologies that allow services to be provided in some way other than face-to-face.[190] Normal check-ins and phone calls for the purposes of scheduling would likely not qualify as service delivery.

I will admit, I sometimes find this requirement a little laughable. It is not as if clients who are receiving therapy by phone are not aware that they are using the phone. But, the underlying reason for the law makes sense: clients need to understand the risks and limitations of the technology being used. We are likely to understand those risks and limitations as they relate to mental health service delivery far better than the clients do. So, as the *Cobbs v. Grant* ruling described, clients need information from us to make a truly informed decision as to whether to participate in technology-assisted services.

Privacy practices

For those therapists and organizations covered by HIPAA (and not all are – see the discussion of HIPAA in Chapter 9), all clients must be given a copy of the provider's Notice of Privacy Practices, detailing how the therapist safeguards the client's private information. The client should acknowledge in writing that they have received that documentation.[191]

---

[190] California Business and Professions Code sections 2290.5(b) and (c)
[191] Office of Civil Rights, U.S. Department of Health and Human Services: Notice of Privacy Practices

▶ Other common elements of disclosure

There are a number of other commonly-included elements of informed consent. While these are not directly required by state law, the law does require that all mental health professionals practice in keeping with the standards of their professions – so most professionals choose to follow common practices within their professions. There are several sample Informed Consent agreements available through professional associations, and they tend to include the elements below. Note that in many instances, these are required by your Code of Ethics.

Limits of confidentiality

While the "big four" exceptions to confidentiality are commonly known, there are also a number of additional exceptions to confidentiality in California (see Chapter 5, Confidentiality, Privilege, and Exceptions) that should be acknowledged in some form. Some therapists prefer to use general language for these other exceptions (for example, my own informed consent agreement notes that there are "other, rare instances where disclosure is required or permitted by law") while others choose to specifically list them. The first option may be better for the therapist if laws regarding confidentiality change, while the latter may be helpful for clients in understanding that these instances are truly not commonly used.

Defining who is the client

In couple and family work, it is important for both the therapist and those attending therapy to be clear as to who is the client. Is the therapist aiming to produce the best outcome for the couple or family, or for a specific person (or people) within it? These can be very different aims. The new ACA Code of Ethics specifically notes that "In the absence of an agreement to the contrary, the couple or family is considered to be the client."[192] There are also implications here regarding confidentiality. Therapists do not share individual confidences without written consent to do so. If the therapist has made clear in the informed consent agreement that the couple or family is considered to be the client, and that individual statements to the therapist may be shared with the person's partner or family, an individual could not claim later that their confidentiality had been breached by such sharing. For more on this important issue, see *Confidentiality with Couples and Families* in Chapter 5.

Cancellation policy

Clients sometimes need to reschedule or cancel planned sessions. Therapists have a variety of policies for such instances, and having your policy agreed to in writing at the beginning of treatment can spare you from awkward conversations later. Many therapists will charge their full fee if a session is cancelled without enough advance notice (24 or 48 hours are common policies, though some therapists require more or less; there is not a uniform standard here).

My private practice is in Los Angeles, where many clients are in some way tied to the entertainment industry. Here, therapists will sometimes provide added flexibility for clients who may not know whether they are working on a given day until they get a call that morning. Some therapists here choose to charge only a nominal fee for late cancellations if the client reschedules (and attends the rescheduled session) within the same week.

Procedures to be used

An Informed Consent document for an individual practitioner can be fairly specific about the techniques the therapist uses, especially if that therapist has a specialized practice. Clinics and other settings where the same Informed Consent agreement is used for many therapists have to be more general in their descriptions of the services to be offered. In either case, though, the Informed Consent often makes clear that clients always have a right to know what

---

[192] ACA Code of Ethics, subprinciple B.4.b

procedures are being used with them and why they are being used. You may also want to have a more specific discussion in person with each client about the procedures being used, revisiting that conversation whenever appropriate, and document that discussion in the client's record.

The informed consent may be a good place to include discussion about the expected length of treatment. Obviously, some treatment methods allow for more specific prediction of treatment length than others.

Risks and benefits

While a general discussion of the risks and benefits of psychotherapy can be included in a written informed consent document, some therapists also will have more detailed conversations with clients about the specific risks and benefits of that particular therapist's type of treatment for the client's particular problem. Such a discussion, if it occurs, should be documented in the client's file.

Of course, not every possible risk can be known ahead of time for any health care procedure. Your discussion of the potential risks of therapy simply needs to cover those risks that are reasonably foreseeable.

One risk of therapy that *is* foreseeable is simple ineffectiveness. No form of therapy is 100% effective. Clients may benefit from knowing before therapy begins that neither you nor any other therapist can guarantee that treatment will work.

Right of refusal

Clients have complete freedom of choice when it comes to their health care. They are under no obligation to start (or, once started, to continue) treatment with a specific therapist. Even a person ordered by a court, their employer, or another outside entity to receive mental health treatment typically can choose their treatment provider. An Informed Consent document will often specify that a client can discontinue treatment at any time and for any reason.

Communication and emergency practices

Can your clients call you between sessions if they feel it necessary? What about in emergencies? If so, how do you charge for this service? What about email, or texting? In our technological age, it may be easier than ever for clients to reach you, which raises concerns about both confidentiality and professional boundaries. You may want to spell out in your Informed Consent agreement precisely how you handle issues like between-session calls, emails, texts, and the like. You may also want to spell out how the client should proceed in a mental health emergency, particularly those where you are not immediately available.

Some therapists who maintain presences on Facebook, Twitter, or other social media use their informed consent documents to describe the nature of their social media relationships. The ACA Code of Ethics requires therapists who use social media to discuss social media as part of informed consent.[193] Clients will naturally be curious about you and your life, but the ACA Code of Ethics requires counselors to keep their personal and professional social media presences separated, so as to avoid confusing clients about the nature of the therapeutic relationship. For all mental health professionals, becoming Facebook "friends" with clients, following clients on Twitter, or connecting with clients through LinkedIn, Instagram, and other social media can raise concerns about confidentiality and multiple relationships, and so is generally discouraged.

Any discussion of communication practices also provides you an opportunity to discuss your rules and practices regarding requests for records (see Chapter 5, Confidentiality, Privilege, and Exceptions).

Billing practices

In order to bill a client's insurance for services, a therapist must send the insurer information about the service provided, the client's diagnosis, and sometimes, additional information. While it is possible to make arrangements for this through a separate Release of Information (see Chapter 5, Confidentiality, Privilege, and Exceptions),

---

[193] ACA Code of Ethics, subprinciple H.6.b

many therapists include information on their interactions with insurance companies in the Informed Consent agreement.

This is also a convenient place to include some information about what happens when clients are unable to pay their fees. The ACA and CAMFT Codes of Ethics specifically addresses this issue, noting that it is ethical to terminate for nonpayment as long as this is done in a manner that is clinically appropriate.[194] However, a therapist should make reasonable efforts to address the issue first. Offering a payment plan, or even reducing the fee, may help the client to remain in therapy. If this is not possible, the client should be referred to any available local low-fee clinics. A therapist cannot refuse to make referrals or withhold treatment records simply because a client has an unpaid balance. As a last resort, therapists may make use of collection agencies to collect unpaid balances from clients. Therapists who do so may want to make note of this in their informed consent agreement.

Therapist background

State law encourages, but does not require, LMFTs to provide clients with detailed statements of their "experience, education, specialties, professional orientation, and any other information deemed appropriate."[195] This does not need to be prior to the beginning of therapy. This encouragement is not included in state law for the other mental health professions.

Wilcoxon et al. similarly advocate the use of a "Professional Disclosure Statement" that can include a great deal of additional information on a therapist's training, background, philosophy, treatment model, and any other relevant information.[196] While that text is also focused on LMFTs, again, providing clients with such information is in keeping with the general principles of informed consent. It would qualify as a best practice for therapists of all types.

---

[194] ACA Code of Ethics subprinciple A.11.c; CAMFT Code of Ethics subprinciple 1.3.4

[195] California Business and Professions Code section 4980.55

[196] Wilcoxon, A., Remley, T. P. Jr., & Gladding, S. T. (2012). *Ethical, Legal, and Professional Issues in the Practice of Marriage and Family Therapy (updated 5th edition)*. Upper Saddle River, NJ: Pearson Education.

Expectations of clients

The discussion of a client's rights and responsibilities in therapy does not need to be limited to their legal rights and responsibilities. You may also want to include discussions about your clinical expectations of the client. These may include expectations regarding the frequency of sessions, client behavior in session, and the client's role relative to the therapist (that is, do you as a therapist take on an expert role with the client, or do you expect the therapy relationship to be more collaborative in nature?).

▶ Verbal versus written consent

> **Consent for mental health services is typically provided in writing.** While the law appears to allow for verbal consent in most instances, in some cases consent **must** be in writing.

California law generally does not specify whether consent for mental health treatment should be in writing or whether verbal consent is sufficient. While the ACA Code of Ethics specifies that counselors need to review the rights and responsibilities of clients and therapists "in writing and verbally,"[197] the codes of ethics of AAMFT, CAMFT, and NASW are not specific as to whether the informed consent process should be verbal or in writing. This would seem to allow for a verbal consent process, which is necessary for those clients who cannot read or who need information about therapy to be translated to their native language. (It can easily be argued that the ACA Code also does allow for this when appropriate). Still, most practitioners generally use a written consent form that each client signs, so there will be no dispute later about what a client was informed of prior to the beginning of treatment. Regardless of how consent is obtained, it should be documented in writing in the client's file.

There are some instances where written consent is necessary. For example, any person bringing a minor in for any form of medical care who is not the minor's parent or guardian but is consenting to the minor's treatment must complete a Caregiver's Authorization Affidavit.[198] This form, discussed again in Chapter 6 on Working with Minors, is not an informed consent agreement by itself, but rather is a way for the adult to attest in writing that they are legally able to consent for the minor's treatment.

Marriage and family therapists should note that the professional ethics codes of counselors and MFTs specifically require **written** informed consent prior to audiotaping or videotaping clients,

---

[197] ACA Code of Ethics subprinciple A.2.a
[198] I've provided a sample Caregiver's Authorization Affidavit for you here: www.bencaldwell.com/extras/caregivers-authorization-affidavit.pdf

or allowing third parties to observe sessions.[199] The ACA Code of Ethics also includes some instances where written informed consent is needed, such as when transferring records to third parties.[200]

---

[199] AAMFT Code of Ethics subprinciple 1.12; ACA Code of Ethics subprinciples B.6.c and B.6.d; CAMFT Code of Ethics subprinciple 1.5.4
[200] ACA Code of Ethics subprinciple B.6.g

▶ Informed consent with minors

> **Parents typically sign an informed consent agreement on behalf of their children. However, minors as young as 12 can consent to their own mental health care in California.** Even when a parent has signed for a minor, therapists often assist the minor in understanding treatment.

Unlike other states, in California minors as young as 12 can independently consent to their own mental health care, so long as the practitioner determines that the minor is mature enough to participate intelligently in treatment.[201] (Trainees and social work associates should be cautious here, as the letter of the law applies only to licensees and to MFT and PCC interns. It is unclear whether minors could independently consent to treatment with a social work associate or with a trainee in any profession.)

One of the ways a therapist might assess whether a minor is capable of consenting to treatment on their own is by going through the informed consent agreement with the minor and evaluating whether the minor is adequately understanding what each part means. If the minor cannot make sense of the limits of confidentiality, for example, the therapist may want to consider whether the minor is capable of participating intelligently in treatment.

Even when the minor shows the maturity needed to consent to treatment on their own, the therapist is required to make contact with the minor's parents unless the therapist can document reasons why that would be detrimental to the minor. There are other areas to consider when working with minors who have consented for treatment on their own. For more about those, see Chapter 6, Working with Minors.

---

[201] California Health & Safety Code section 124260(d)

Assent agreements

For minors too young to consent to treatment on their own, or who legally could do so but are nonetheless covered by a consent form signed by a parent, therapists still engage in an informed consent process. In doing so, they sometimes make use of "Assent agreements." These are not legally binding, but do describe for children (in age-appropriate language) what the therapy process is and how it works. This can alleviate their fears of coming to a therapist's office, and help them understand their role in therapy.

Even when children are too young to read an assent agreement, a therapist can work with the parent or guardian to ensure that the child has an age-appropriate understanding of where they are, who the therapist is, and what they have come to the therapy office for.

5

Confidentiality, Privilege, and Exceptions

In order to allow clients to feel safe in therapy, the law generally protects information about therapy from being shared. However, there are several exceptions, where the good of the public is considered to outweigh the client's right to privacy. Many therapists are aware of the most common exceptions to confidentiality, but even many experienced therapists are unaware that there are more than 20 different situations in which a therapist is either required or allowed to break confidentiality under California law.

▶ Basic principles

For several years, the treatment contract I used in my private practice included this statement: "The therapy office is like Vegas. What happens here stays here." I've switched to using a bit more formal language these days, but the underlying idea is the same: The therapy room must be a private setting, to allow clients to feel safe in sharing parts of their lives that they might otherwise be embarrassed or ashamed to discuss. This, like informed consent, is a fundamental principle of ethical psychotherapy.

While there is meaningful overlap between the two, the terms *confidentiality* and *privilege* mean somewhat different things. **Confidentiality refers to your responsibility as a therapist to keep the process of therapy private**. This is the term used in professional codes of ethics. **Privilege is a specific legal term, and refers to the right of a client** (or whoever holds privilege for them; more on that later) **to keep you from testifying in court about their therapy.**

To you, to your client, and to most of the outside world, confidentiality is usually the key concept. Therapists keep information from therapy confidential, including even the fact that someone even *is* your client.[202] As we will see, there are several exceptions to this general rule.

In a court proceeding, privilege is often the more relevant concept. Communications between a client and therapist are considered *privileged communications* under the law.[203] For this reason, a court cannot force a therapist to share information about therapy in a court proceeding, except in limited circumstances. If a therapist receives a subpoena (a request for information as part of a court proceeding), professional associations typically advise that the therapist consult with the client to see whether the client will consent to releasing the information. If not, the therapist may refuse to give information to the court, known as *asserting privilege*. Such an assertion has to be formally stated, of course; a therapist should not

---

[202] Leslie, D. (1989 July/August). Confidentiality. *The Therapist.*
[203] California Evidence Code section 1014

simply fail to respond to a subpoena (see "Responding to a subpoena" later in this chapter).

There is some functional overlap between these two concepts. For example, section 1024 of the Evidence Code specifies that any information a client shares in therapy that is a threat to property is not covered under therapist-client privilege.[204] This has been interpreted by CAMFT to mean that therapists can break confidentiality if necessary to resolve such a threat.[205] However, **where disclosures are allowed but not required by law, therapists generally err on the side of protecting confidentiality.**[206]

---

[204] California Evidence Code section 1024
[205] Pelchat, Z. (2001 July/August). Legal issues in treating suicidal patients. *The Therapist*.
[206] Leslie, D. (1989 July/August). Confidentiality. *The Therapist*.

▶ Confidentiality and its exceptions

> **Therapists must break confidentiality if the therapist suspects child, elder, or dependent adult abuse, or if a client poses an active danger to themselves or others and less intrusive actions do not remove the danger.** There are many other, lesser-known exceptions.

Confidentiality is recognized across the mental health professions as a cornerstone of ethical psychotherapy. All California psychotherapists are required to learn about confidentiality,[207] and failing to uphold a client's confidentiality can result in action against your license or registration (see Chapter 3, Unprofessional Conduct).[208]

There are a number of exceptions to confidentiality defined in the law. While many therapists are aware of the most common exceptions, you may be surprised at some of the exceptions to confidentiality that come up less often.

As a general rule, any time you are allowed to break confidentiality, you should *just enough information to resolve the problem at hand.*[209] If you are dealing with a threat and need to break confidentiality, you should not reveal any more information about your client than what is necessary to address the immediate threat. If you are reporting abuse, the information you share should only be the information necessary for the abuse report; you would not offer additional information on someone's course of therapy, their treatment goals, or other parenting issues if that information is not relevant to the specific incident of abuse being reported. In this way, we make safety the highest priority but provide as much

---

[207] California Business and Professions Code sections 4980.36(d)(2)(J)(iv) and 4999.33(c)(3)(I), and Council on Social Work Education 2008 Accreditation Standards Educational Policy 2.1.2
[208] California Business and Professions Code sections 4982(m), 4992.3(n), and 4999.90(m)
[209] ACA Code of Ethics subprinciple B.2.e

confidentiality as possible while addressing safety needs. This can be a challenging balance.

Danger to self

Most mental health clinicians will work with at least one patient who is actively considering suicide at some point in their careers. State law requires mental health professionals to receive training in suicide assessment and intervention so that such clients can be properly assessed and treated, ensuring that they do not ultimately hurt themselves.[210]

Bellah v. Greenson

Before this court case, it was actually unclear what a therapist's responsibility was to a client who was contemplating suicide. Of course, we all would work to intervene with the client when they are in the therapy office. But does that responsibility extend beyond the walls of the therapy room? And is it acceptable to warn a friend, a family member, or law enforcement that your client has just shared their suicidal feelings with you in session and now they are on their way home, where you fear they will follow through?

In the case of *Bellah v. Greenson*, the parents of a young woman who had committed suicide by overdosing on pills sued her psychiatrist. The parents argued that the psychiatrist had not taken adequate action to prevent the suicide even though he knew their daughter was a suicide risk. The parents argued that the same principles at work in the *Tarasoff* case (discussed below) applied here.

An appeals court disagreed. They refused to extend the specific provisions of the *Tarasoff* case, which would have required therapists to warn authorities if a client was actively suicidal. However, the court did determine that because of the special relationship between therapist and client, **a therapist does have a responsibility to take reasonable steps to prevent a threatened suicide**. The court ruling

---

[210] California Business and Professions Code sections 4980.36(d)(2)(J)(iv) and 4999.33(c)(3)(I). For social workers, the Council on Social Work Education 2008 Accreditation Standards requires training consistent with the NASW Code of Ethics, and that Code demands appropriate intervention in risk (subprinciple 1.02).

did not say what those "reasonable steps" would be, leaving that question up to the standards of "good medical practice" – that is, the standard of care.[211]

Intervening with a suicidal client

Today, there are a number of well-developed and commonly used suicide assessment protocols available. Most focus on issues like the presence and detail of a suicide plan, the intent to follow through with that plan, and the availability of means to carry out the plan. If you determine in assessing your client that they pose a danger to themselves, you must intervene in an effort to help them. This can involve breaking confidentiality if necessary. Depending on the immediacy and severity of the threat, and the location of the client, you have a number of interventions available to you; note that our focus is on laws, so **this is not a complete list**. Remember too that in any threat situation, you want to use the least intrusive means you can use that will actually resolve the threat. This requires seeking out a careful balance between safety and confidentiality, granting as much confidentiality as is possible while keeping the person safe.

Safety planning. In the past, many therapists have used written agreements with clients where the client agreed not to hurt themselves in any way prior to the next meeting with the therapist. Such agreements, often referred to as "no harm contracts," have largely fallen out of favor in the field. For one thing, they are not contracts in any legally enforceable way; if your client completed such a contract and then went on to attempt suicide anyway, it is not as though the therapist would then sue the client for breach of contract. Another reason these have fallen out of favor is that they may actually hurt a therapist's defense if the therapist is alleged to have not acted sufficiently to prevent a suicide. If you believed your client was at risk for suicide – which the mere presence of a no-harm contract would suggest – and you made no additional effort to ensure their safety beyond having them sign a form saying they would not harm themselves, you might be seen as not having done enough.

Of course, not all clients having thoughts of suicide need constant care or other intrusive forms of intervention. For clients who

---

[211] *Bellah v. Greenson*, 81 Cal. App. 3d 614 (1978)

are thinking about suicide but assessed to be low risk, therapists are often now using **safety plans**.

A safety plan is a written agreement where the client commits to taking a number of specific actions before doing anything that would be harmful to themselves. While safety plans come in many forms, these actions often follow a stepwise progression; for example, a client who starts thinking about suicide while at home might have agreed to first reach out to a friend or family member. If that friend or family member is not available or contacting them is not helpful to the client, the client has agreed to then call the therapist or therapist's clinic. If the therapist or another person from the clinic is not available, or if that contact is insufficient, the client might commit to then calling the local crisis hotline.

It is important to note that such safety plans are typically used with clients who pose low suicide risk. In essence, they are a protective measure just in case a client's symptoms worsen. If the client does wind up making use of any part of the safety plan, the therapist is likely to thoroughly reassess at the next session whether a more intrusive level of intervention is needed.

Care of a loved one. If a client is not a severe enough risk to warrant hospitalization, but enough of a concern that you feel they should be in the presence of other people, you may want to ask the client's friends or family members for assistance. While the *Bellah v. Greenson* ruling would suggest that breaking confidentiality is acceptable when informing a client's family members of a suicide risk can help them protect the client, clients are often willing to either make contact with family members themselves, or voluntarily grant permission for you to do so, such that there is no breach of confidentiality.

Voluntary hospitalization. If a client's suicidality poses such a risk that they are an imminent danger to themselves, hospitalization is necessary. Once it has been established that hospitalization is needed, the choice for your client comes down to whether this hospitalization will be voluntary or involuntary. Clients are likely to prefer voluntary hospitalization.

Involuntary hospitalization. If a client poses an immediate threat to themselves, and is unable or unwilling to receive appropriate care, a psychotherapist may initiate the process of involuntary hospitalization described in section 5150 of the California Welfare and Institutions Code.[212] (You might have heard therapists using that number as a verb. A person who is involuntarily hospitalized is sometimes referred to as having been "fifty-one-fiftied.") Note here that a therapist can begin the process, but most therapists cannot actually *invoke* an involuntary hospitalization. Only a licensed physician or another professional specifically authorized by their county can make the final determination as to whether someone will be hospitalized against their will.

Once a person has been admitted to the hospital under section 5150, they may be initially held for up to three days. That is why involuntary hospitalizations are also referred to as "72-hour holds." Most 72-hour holds are actually much shorter; a person hospitalized against their will may be discharged as soon as they have met with a physician who has determined the patient is no longer a threat. In many instances, a 72-hour hold actually lasts less than a day before the patient is released. At the same time, a 72-hour hold can actually be longer than three days if it occurs over a weekend or holiday at facilities permitted by the state to not count weekends and holidays toward the 72-hour limit.[213]

If, however, the 72-hour hold has elapsed and the patient still poses a threat to themselves, the patient can be held for up to 14 more days.[214] If the patient is still an active danger to themselves at the end of that 14-day hold, they may be hospitalized for up to 14 *more* days.[215] Beyond that time frame, they must be released unless they have voluntarily agreed to continued treatment, have been recommended to be placed on conservatorship, or present an active danger to others.[216]

---

[212] California Welfare and Institutions Code section 5150
[213] California Welfare and Institutions Code section 5151
[214] California Welfare and Institutions Code section 5250
[215] California Welfare and Institutions Code sections 5257(b)(2) and 5260
[216] California Welfare and Institutions Code section 5260(b)

Danger to others

Clients regularly come to therapy expressing feelings of anger or a desire for aggression – indeed, that is often what clients come to therapy to resolve. It is vital to understand the difference between a client who is simply expressing anger and one who presents a risk of violence.

Tarasoff v. California Board of Regents

If you are reading this text as part of a Law & Ethics class, you may already be familiar with the *Tarasoff* case. It involved a young woman, Tatiana Tarasoff, who was studying as an undergraduate at the University of California-Berkeley when she met Prosenjit Poddar, a graduate student. Poddar pursued a romantic relationship with Tarasoff, and gradually became obsessed with her. When she attempted to break off their relationship, he began having violent fantasies about her. He sought therapy through the university while Tarasoff was spending the summer with a family member, and he told the therapist about his violent fantasies. The therapist notified campus police, who picked up Poddar and then released him when he promised to stay away from Tarasoff. He dropped out of therapy, and when Tarasoff returned that fall, he stabbed her to death.[217]

Tatiana's parents sued the Psychologist who had provided Poddar's therapy and the university, arguing that their daughter should have been warned of the danger she faced upon returning to campus. California courts ruled that **therapists have a duty to protect reasonably identifiable victims of a dangerous or threatening client.** "The confidential character of patient-psychotherapist communications must yield to the extent that disclosure is essential to avert danger to others," the court wrote, adding famously, "The protective privilege ends where the public peril begins."[218]

---

[217] *Tarasoff v. Regents of the University of California*, 17 Cal. 3d 425, 442 (1976)
[218] *Tarasoff v. Regents of the University of California*, 17 Cal. 3d 425, 442 (1976), p. 10

As with suicidal clients, it is vital to effectively assess the potential danger posed by your client and respond appropriately to that level of danger. If a client merely expresses anger at another person, but no intent to harm them, their assurances may be all you need. If they do not appear dangerous during session but you worry that they may become dangerous, a safety plan may be appropriate. But if the client leaves your office presenting an imminent danger to others, you must act to resolve the threat. Your available options for intervening are different if your client poses an imminent danger to *specific, reasonably identifiable others* as opposed to presenting a *general danger* to anyone who happens to be nearby. Again, remember that our focus is on California law, so the list below is not a complete list of possible interventions for a dangerous client.

However you choose to intervene, remember again that any time a therapist breaks confidentiality, even when the law allows or requires the therapist to do so, the therapist should only provide the minimum information necessary to meet their legal requirement. Do not share any details of the client's therapy that are not relevant to the immediate threat.

Reasonably identifiable victims. If your client poses an imminent danger to reasonably identifiable victims, then you must act to protect those victims in accordance with the *Tarasoff* ruling. This may mean warning the victims directly, contacting law enforcement, and any other steps necessary to eliminate the threat. It is important to remember here that **yours is a duty to *protect*, not necessarily a "duty to warn."** While warning the potential victim typically is a necessary step in protecting them from a dangerous client, it is not always possible or helpful. Consider the example of a client who is known to be a gang member, and tells you of his plans to kill a rival gang member. If you warn the potential victim of this threat, you may actually *provoke* violence from the rival gang. Legislation passed in 2012 clarified that therapists' duty in such cases is the *protection*, and not necessarily the warning, of potential victims. Therapists must take "reasonable efforts" to notify intended victims *and* law enforcement when a client poses a threat to reasonably identifiable victims. This matched instructions that California courts had been giving to juries in such cases for years.[219] The statute notes that if you make reasonable efforts to warn the victim and communicate with law enforcement about the threat, you are immune from liability.[220]

The issue has been further complicated by a 2004 California court ruling in the case of *Ewing v. Goldstein*, which found that a therapist should treat communications from a client's family member (about the client posing a threat) similarly to how they would treat such statements coming directly from the client.[221]

Following mass shootings in Newtown, CT, and Isla Vista, CA, legislators re-examined the laws surrounding when potentially dangerous clients of mental health professionals should be allowed to buy or possess guns. A California law that took effect January 1, 2014, specified that a person who communicated a "serious threat of physical violence against a reasonably identifiable victim or victims" to a licensed therapist should not be allowed to possess a gun for five years unless a court grants permission for them to do so.[222] **A licensed therapist whose client communicates such a threat must report that threat to local law enforcement within 24 hours**, so that local law enforcement can inform federal authorities and the gun possession ban can take effect.[223] Of course, in many such cases you would already be informing local law enforcement immediately of such a threat, as you carry out your duty to protect the possible victims. However, even if you are able to adequately protect the possible victims without immediately notifying law enforcement, under this law you still must make them aware of the threat within 24 hours. Since this law is written in such a way that it applies only to communications from the client of a *licensed* therapist, you should consult your supervisor and an attorney if you are a registrant or trainee dealing with such a threat. In light of the *Ewing v. Goldstein* ruling noted above, you should also consult an attorney if you learned about the threat through a third party such as the client's family member.

---

[219] Senate Bill 1134 (Yee), 2012
[220] California Civil Code section 43.92(b)
[221] *Ewing v Goldstein*, 15 Cal Rptr. 3d 864 (Cal. Ct. App. 2004). An APA brief on the case can be read at www.apa.org/about/offices/ogc/amicus/ewing.aspx
[222] California Welfare and Institutions Code section 8100
[223] California Welfare and Institutions Code section 8105(c)

General danger to others. If your client is in such a distressed or aggressive state that they pose a general danger to others, but there is no reasonably identifiable victim to protect, then you may act to intervene with the client in accordance with section 5150 of the Welfare and Institutions Code. As is the case with a suicidal client, **those who pose a general danger to others may be involuntarily hospitalized for up to 72 hours.**[224] Once the 72-hour hold has elapsed, the patient can be held for up to 14 more days if they still pose a danger to others.[225] If the patient remains a danger to others at the end of that 14-day hold, they may be hospitalized for up to 180 *more* days for additional treatment if they are determined by a court or jury to present a continued risk.[226] At the end of that 180 days, the process can be renewed with a new court certification that the patient continues to present a danger to others.[227]

Danger to property

One of the strongest arguments in favor of breaking confidentiality over a threat to property is the risk that when property is damaged, destroyed, or stolen, a person might accidentally be hurt in the process. If your client were a burglar and they told you what house they would be robbing tonight, the simple fact that the client does not intend to harm any person does not mean that either the client or those living in the house are safe. If the client was wrong about the house being empty, and a physical confrontation occurred, you may wish you had intervened.

Section 1024 of the California Evidence Code says that the therapist-patient privilege does not apply if a client, because of a mental or emotional condition, poses a threat to threat to themselves or the person *or property* of another.[228] This has been interpreted to mean that psychotherapists are allowed, but not required, to

---

[224] California Welfare and Institutions Code section 5150
[225] California Welfare and Institutions Code section 5250
[226] California Welfare and Institutions Code section 5300
[227] California Welfare and Institutions Code section 5304(b)
[228] California Evidence Code section 1024

communicate with law enforcement or others to reduce or remove the threat.[229]

If you do choose to break confidentiality to prevent a danger to property, the law is not specific as to who you should share information with. This flexibility allows you to break confidentiality – as minimally as possible, remember – to whomever is best positioned to resolve the threat. This could mean the property owner, a family member of the person making the threat, law enforcement, or anyone else you identify as needing to be informed in order to eliminate the danger.

Child, elder, or dependent adult abuse

California law protects vulnerable populations from abuse. Therapists are required to break confidentiality if they develop reasonable suspicion that a child, elder, or dependent adult is the victim of abuse. For more information on child abuse reporting, see Chapter 6, Working with Minors. For more information on elder and dependent adult abuse, see Chapter 7, Working with Elders and Dependent Adults.

Releases of information

Of course, you are allowed to break confidentiality if you have been given permission by the client to do so. A written request from a client to share information from therapy with a specific third party is called a *release of information*. Most agencies have release forms for their employees, and mental health professional associations make sample release forms available as well.

If you work in a setting that is covered under HIPAA, you may be interested in knowing that HIPAA allows health care providers across multiple settings to share information about a client even without a written release for the purposes of treatment planning.[230] As

---

[229] Pelchat, Z. (2001 July/August). Legal issues in treating suicidal patients. *The Therapist.*
[230] Code of Federal Regulations title 45 section 164.506. A useful summary of the HIPAA privacy rules can be found at www.hhs.gov/ocr/privacy/hipaa/understanding/summary/index.html

a practical matter, however, most settings still require the written form. If nothing else, this provides assurance that the person who would be receiving the information actually is actively involved in the client's treatment.

Other exceptions to confidentiality

In addition to the common exceptions outlined above, state and federal law define several additional exceptions to confidentiality. While these are not commonly used, it is helpful to know them and to share with your clients that these are additional instances where disclosure of information may be required. **Other situations where therapists are <u>required</u> to break confidentiality if asked to do so include those on the following list:**[231]

- Court order
- Investigation by a board, commission, or administrative agency
- Subpoena from a court (i.e., from a judge – see "Responding to a subpoena" later in this chapter)
- Lawful request from an arbitrator or arbitration panel
- Search warrant
- Coroner's investigation, when the person whose death is being investigated is the client
- Request for records from a client or client's representative (there are limited times when you can justify not turning over records; see "Client requests for records" later in this chapter)

In addition to these, **there are other instances where a therapist is <u>allowed</u>, but not mandated, to break confidentiality:**[232]

- Communicating with other providers, health plans, or facilities for the purposes of diagnosis or treatment
- Determining responsibility for payment and for payment to be made

---

[231] California Civil Code section 56.10(b)
[232] California Civil Code section 56.10(c)

- To a billing, claims management, medical data processing, or other administrative process
- To an official review group for quality control
- To a licensing or accreditation body for the health care provider
- As part of a coroner's investigation when the person whose death is being investigated is not the client
- For research purposes
- Related to employment, if the information comes from employment-related health care services, such as when a client has made their mental condition the focus of a lawsuit against their employer or if the client's fitness for their job is impacted

These are just a sampling. There are a total of 21 instances where a therapist is allowed, but not required, to break confidentiality in this section of state law. While you may initially think these don't matter – after all, your ethics codes still require you to maintain confidentiality – bear in mind that ethics codes usually include an exception for times when breaking confidentiality is required or allowed by law.[233] You can then use your professional judgment and consultation with colleagues, supervisors, and an attorney, as you see fit, to determine whether disclosure of confidential information is warranted. As previously mentioned, when disclosure is allowed but not required, therapists tend to prefer upholding confidentiality.[234]

---

[233] AAMFT Code of Ethics subprinciple 2.2; ACA Code of Ethics subprinciple B.1.c; CAMFT Code of Ethics subprinciple 2.1; NASW Code of Ethics subprinciple 1.07(e)
[234] Leslie, D. (1989 July/August). Confidentiality. *The Therapist.*

▶ Privilege

Communications between a client and a therapist are considered to be privileged communications under the law.[235] This essentially means that the state considers the privacy of these conversations to be of the utmost importance, so much so that the content of therapy cannot even be used in most court proceedings unless the client, or a judge, allows it.

Just as there are exceptions to confidentiality, there are also exceptions to privilege. As we discussed above, client threats to property are not considered privileged communications. Other exceptions apply as well.

Note that the discussion here applies to situations where it is your *client* who is involved in a court proceeding. If *you* are the person being sued, the rules are a bit different, and you should utilize the services of an attorney regarding issues of privilege.

Holders of privilege

Clients generally are holders of their own privilege.[236] That is, they can determine on their own whether they would like to allow for confidential information from their therapy to be revealed in a court process. This is particularly important for therapists to be aware of with minors; **even minors are typically holders of their own privilege**, though as we will see below, minors are not always free to choose on their own whether to waive it.

In some instances, the court may appoint someone to be responsible for the client's decisions regarding privilege, particularly if the client is a minor. This person is called a *guardian ad litem.*

---

[235] California Evidence Code section 1014
[236] California Evidence Code section 1013

Asserting privilege

As a mental health provider, you can refuse to release information on the grounds that any communications between a client and a psychotherapist are considered privileged communications under the law. This is called "asserting privilege," and you can assert privilege without revealing even whether the person involved in the court case is a client of yours. However, you cannot assert privilege if your client asks, or a judge demands, that privilege be waived.

Asserting privilege does not mean simply failing to respond to a request for records, though. It must be done formally, and is often necessary if you receive a request for records from a judge or an attorney.

Responding to a subpoena

Courts and the attorneys who represent clients often request records of psychotherapy, or even request the therapist to appear in court, as part of a court case. Such a request is called a **subpoena**. (If you are not familiar with that term, it's pronounced suh-PEE-nuh.) At first, it may be difficult to tell whether the request has come from a judge or from a private attorney, but the source of the subpoena is important. If it comes from a judge, you *must* comply, as it has the power of a court order. If it comes from a private attorney, and you do not have your client's authorization to release records, it may actually be a *violation* of the law for you to turn over the records requested in the subpoena.

You essentially have three options when served with a subpoena:[237]

1. Assert privilege
2. Object to the subpoena
3. Comply with the request for records or court appearance

---

[237] Jensen, D. (2007 November/December). Diagnosing a subpoena for validity. *The Therapist.*

Unless you know that privilege has been waived or a judge has determined that privilege does not apply, asserting privilege is an appropriate default position for a therapist to take.[238] What you should *not* do is simply fail to respond to a subpoena. If you do not respond to a lawfully issued subpoena, you can be held in contempt of court, and fined or even jailed.

Objecting to the subpoena may be appropriate if there is something wrong with the subpoena itself or with how it was delivered. In most instances, a subpoena must be delivered to you in person. In many instances, it must come with supporting documentation. It may be useful to consult an attorney who can help determine whether it is appropriate to object to a subpoena.[239]

When you receive any subpoena related to a client's therapy, it will be useful to consult with both your own attorney and the client (or the client's attorney or representative). The client or their attorney will determine whether to waive privilege when it comes to their treatment.

If the subpoena is valid and it either comes from a judge or your client agrees to waive privilege, your responsibility is to comply with the subpoena, by producing the requested records, appearing in court at the requested time, or both.

Waiving privilege

Most clients can choose to *waive privilege*, thus allowing a therapist to discuss their therapy in a court proceeding, if they wish. However, courts do not always defer to the client who wants to waive privilege. Judges may block a client's request to waive privilege if the judge believes doing so is not in the client's best interest, particularly if the client is a minor.

In any case, **it is never up to the therapist to determine whether privilege should be waived**. It is always the choice of the client, the client's guardian (including guardians appointed by the court), another court appointee, or a judge. If a client instructs you

---

[238] California Evidence Code section 1015
[239] Jensen, D. (2007 November/December). Diagnosing a subpoena for validity. *The Therapist.*

that they are waiving privilege, you should document and follow their instruction.

Exceptions to privilege

The law defines a number of exceptions to psychotherapist-client privilege, including (among others):

- If a client, anyone making a claim on the client's behalf, or a beneficiary of the client raises the client's mental or emotional state as an issue in a court proceeding.[240]
- If the client sought the therapist's services for the purpose of planning or committing a crime, or to avoid being arrested for a crime after the fact.[241]
- If the client is a danger to themselves, to others, or to property, and disclosure of that information is necessary to prevent the threat.[242] See "threats to property" above.
- If the client is under age 16 and is the victim of a crime, and the therapist believes that disclosing that information is in the child's best interest.[243]

A client's death does *not* create an exception to privilege, as the client's representative can still claim privilege on their behalf. However, once a client has died, any information the client told their therapist about how they wanted their property distributed is not subject to privilege.[244]

---

[240] California Evidence Code section 1016
[241] California Evidence Code section 1018
[242] California Evidence Code section 1024
[243] California Evidence Code section 1027
[244] California Evidence Code section 1021

▶ Maintaining confidentiality

Now that you are familiar with all of the exceptions to confidentiality, let us return to your core responsibility: maintaining it. In spite of the high number of specific exceptions to confidentiality under state law, those are still exceptions; unless one or more of them clearly apply, you must keep all information from therapy sessions confidential.[245] Here we examine your responsibilities to maintain privacy of treatment records, and how to maintain confidentiality appropriately in couple/family and group treatment contexts.

Record-keeping

You may have noticed that this book does not contain any guidance on the specific content of therapy notes. This is because state law simply requires that you keep treatment records consistent with "sound clinical judgment [and] the standards of the profession,"[246] and the standard of care for record-keeping changes over time. Recall from our earlier discussion of the *standard of care* that books and journal articles, in addition to the practices of colleagues, can offer strong guidance on the standard of care within your field. For information on how to document therapy, a number of popular texts are available, including *Documenting Psychotherapy*[247] and *The Psychotherapy Documentation Primer*.[248] Specifically for LMFTs, *Mastering Competencies in Family Therapy: A Practical Approach to Theory and*

---

[245] California Business and Professions Code sections 4982(m), 4992.3(n), and 4999.90(m)

[246] California Business and Professions Code sections 4982(v), 4992.3(t), and 4999.90(v)

[247] Moline, M. E., Williams, G. T., & Austin, K. M. (1997). *Documenting Psychotherapy: Essentials for Mental Health Practitioners*. Thousand Oaks, CA: Sage.

[248] Wiger, D. E. (2012). *The Psychotherapy Documentation Primer (3rd edition)*. Hoboken, NJ: John Wiley & Sons.

Clinical Case Documentation[249] also offers a wealth of resources and examples.

Client requests for records

Clients are typically entitled to review or receive a copy of their treatment records if they wish. If a client requests their records, you must comply within five days if the client simply is asking to inspect their records, and within 15 days if they are requesting a copy of their records.[250] You cannot refuse a client's request for records simply because they owe you fees for past sessions.[251] However, you can require clients to pay for reasonable clerical costs of locating the client's file and making it available, including the cost of copies. You also can provide a summary of the client's record, rather than the full record, if you prefer.[252] If you prepare a summary, it must be made available within 10 days of the client's request.

If the client, upon reviewing their records, sees something they think is incorrect or incomplete, they have the right to submit a statement of up to 250 words that you must add to the client record.[253]

If you believe that your client would suffer negative consequences from seeing their treatment records, you can refuse their request to see their records. However, this rule comes with a number of additional requirements. If you do choose to refuse a client's request for records, you must (1) document within the client's record the date of their request and your reasons for refusing it, including the specific negative consequences you think would happen to the client if they were to see their records; (2) inform the client that you are refusing their request, and of their right to designate another mental health professional who could review the records on their

---

[249] Gehart, D. R. (2014). *Mastering Competencies in Family Therapy: A Practical Approach to Theory and Clinical Case Documentation.* Belmont, CA: Brooks/Cole.
[250] California Health and Safety Code section 123110(a)
[251] California Health and Safety Code section 123110(j)
[252] California Health and Safety Code section 123130(a)
[253] California Health and Safety Code section 123111

behalf; and (3) make the records available to the licensed or registered mental health professional of the client's choosing.[254]

How long to keep records

As I mentioned in Chapter 3, as of January 1, 2015, therapists are expected to retain treatment records for at least 7 years after the last professional contact with clients who are adults. If treatment involved a minor, the therapist should retain the records until the minor turns 25 (that is, 7 years after their 18th birthday).[255] You can choose to retain records for longer than this if you wish; the law simply provides a *minimum* amount of time for which records must be kept.

The current *statute of limitations* – that is, the amount of time the BBS has to take action against you based on an act you are alleged to have committed in your therapy practice – is 7 years for most violations, and 10 years for violations involving sexual misconduct. For acts involving sexual contact with a minor, the BBS can act for 3 years *from the time that they first learn about the act* – no matter how long it has been since the act occurred – as long as there is corroborating evidence. For other violations involving minors, the clock does not start on these time periods until the minor turns 18.[256]

Since treatment records can be important in a therapist's defense against charges of wrongdoing, many therapists choose to retain their records for 10 years following the conclusion of treatment. Some therapists who work with minors retain their records for at least 10 years following the time the minor turns 18.

Storage and disposal of records

In today's digital age, records can be retained for much longer periods of time if the therapist or therapist's employer chooses. State law does not define a maximum length of time to retain records. For as

---

[254] California Health and Safety Code section 123115(b)
[255] California Business and Professions Code sections 4980.49(a), 4993(a), and 4999.75(a)
[256] California Business and Professions Code sections 4982.05 and 4990.32

long as records are maintained, they must be secured to prevent the disclosure of confidential information.

State law specifies that health care records must be secured, but does not specify *how* records must be secured. As we will discuss in Chapter 9 (Technology), federal laws also purposefully do not specify specific methods of securing files, because the digital technology for creating and securing files is changing so quickly. Federal law instead requires that security practices be adequate and that they be *regularly reviewed and updated*, understanding that the needs of different providers will vary.

When the time comes for records to be disposed of, you cannot simply throw paper files in the trash. As is the case with any California business, you must dispose of records by shredding or other means that protect clients' confidentiality.[257]

Confidentiality with couples and families

As you can imagine, issues of confidentiality are more complicated when you work with couples or families. While you have a legal responsibility to maintain your clients' confidentiality, they have no such responsibility to each other. Furthermore, you have to make difficult decisions as a therapist when it comes to keeping what one family member tells you confidential from another.

When working with couples or families, some therapists choose a *no-secrets policy*. With this understanding with the clients, everyone agrees that any information any individual in the family shares with the therapist – even if other family members are not around at the time – is "fair game" for the therapist to bring up in a future family session. This keeps the therapist from being put in an awkward position if one family member, speaking with the therapist by phone or on an individual basis, acknowledges an affair, substance use, or some other issue that is impacting the family but that other family members may not be aware of.

Other therapists prefer a *limited-secrets policy*, where the therapist does keep some information learned from individuals secret from the others, even when the focus of treatment is the couple or family. Some therapists prefer this kind of policy because they feel it

---

[257] California Civil Code section 1798.81

allows for clients to be more open in the assessment stage of therapy, particularly around issues like intimate partner violence that may be easier to discuss when a family member is alone with the therapist than when in front of an abusive partner or the couple's children.

Neither of these policies is inherently right or wrong; this has been an issue of debate for some time in family work, and state law would allow for either kind of policy. Whatever policy on secrets you choose for couple and family work, **each member of the couple or family should agree to that policy in writing.** Confidentiality is an individual right, and the ethics codes of many of the major mental health associations covered in this text specifically require addressing the confidentiality of each individual client within a couple or family treatment context.[258] As part of this policy, you may ask family members to commit to keeping each other's confidentiality outside of the therapy room, though there is no legal requirement for them to do so.

Confidentiality in group therapy

As with couples and families, members of a therapy group are not bound to maintain each other's confidentiality outside of the group setting. Indeed, it is common for the sharing of personal information in session to lead group members to become friends outside of the therapy room. While this can be good for clients in building their social support, it also can raise questions about group boundaries.

You do have a responsibility as a therapist to maintain the confidentiality of all group members. If you are running a therapy group, it may be helpful to regularly review the expectations of group members, including boundaries on sharing anything from the group with outsiders. Some professional ethics codes encourage regularly revisiting issues of confidentiality in any therapy setting,[259] and some specifically address the importance of clarifying confidentiality in a

---

[258] AAMFT Code of Ethics subprinciple 2.2; ACA Code of Ethics subprinciple B.4.b; NASW Code of Ethics subprinciple 1.07(f)
[259] AAMFT Code of Ethics subprinciple 2.1; ACA Code of Ethics subprinciple B.1.d; NASW Code of Ethics subprinciple 1.07(e)

group treatment setting.[260] You may even choose to set a policy where those who violate the confidentiality of the group may be asked to leave the group.

Confidentiality in the Internet age

Maintaining confidentiality can become far more difficult if you are working with clients via phone or videoconference, issues we will tackle in Chapter 9 (Technology). Even when you are providing services in person, the Internet has created interesting new concerns about client confidentiality.

Web sites like Yelp, Angie's List, Health Grades, and many more allow consumers to post their reviews of professionals in a wide variety of fields. This can make for difficult decision-making where confidentiality is concerned. What happens if a client posts a negative review of you on one of these sites? Even worse, what if the person posting about negative experiences with you in therapy isn't a client, and never was?

Remember from the beginning of this chapter that it is typically *your* responsibility to maintain confidentiality, even as it applies to something as basic as whether a person has been your client, and even if the client does not seem concerned about keeping therapy confidential. When someone posts about your clinical work online, regardless of whether they are a client or just pretending to be, that should not be taken as their permission for you to talk openly about them or to respond to their comments.

Most therapists presented with such a situation will choose simply to not respond. Some, however, choose to be a bit more proactive. By registering with such sites and controlling their directory information (basic information like your address and phone number), therapists sometimes have the opportunity to add a statement to their listing outlining the limits of confidentiality and explaining that they cannot respond to any comments posted there, even to say that someone wasn't actually their client.

---

[260] AAMFT Code of Ethics subprinciple 2.2; ACA Code of Ethics subprinciple B.4.a; CAMFT Code of Ethics subprinciple 2.7; NASW Code of Ethics subprinciple 1.07(f)

6

Working with Minors

California has an extensive array of laws to balance three sometimes-competing needs: minors' need for developmentally appropriate autonomy in decision-making, caregivers' needs to have input in their children's care, and the state's interest in making sure that all children are protected from abuse. This chapter is focused exclusively on the California state laws that psychotherapists will most commonly need to be aware of in working with children.

▶ Restrictions on work with minors

Providing psychotherapy to minors (individuals under age 18) is within the scope of practice of all the psychotherapy professions, including clinical social work, professional clinical counseling, and marriage and family therapy. However, there are two key restrictions in state law for working with minors.

Ban on sexual orientation change efforts

As you learned in Chapter 3 (Unprofessional Conduct), it can be considered general unprofessional conduct for a licensed or registered therapist to attempt to change a minor's sexual orientation through therapy. This law was very carefully worded so as to ban the therapies that seek such changes, without hindering conversations that therapists legitimately should be having with adolescent clients about their developing romantic relationships and sexual identities.

LPCC limitation on working with families

Professional clinical counselors can work with minors. However, because working with minors necessarily involves working with families (see "Involving family members" later in this chapter), clinical counselors wishing to work with minors must be aware of the unique restrictions in their scope of practice related to assessing or treating families.

Unlike the other psychotherapy professions, Licensed Professional Clinical Counselors (LPCCs) have specific restrictions on their ability to work with couples and families. In order to *assess or treat* a couple or family, an LPCC must complete the following education and supervised experience, above and beyond the requirements for licensure:

- 6 semester units or 9 quarter units of coursework in couple and family therapy, or a named specialization in couple and family therapy on their degree
- 500 hours supervised experience with couples, families, and children (these can be gained during, and counted

toward, the 3,000 hours of supervised post-degree experience required for licensure)
- 6 hours of continuing education on couple and family work in each renewal cycle[261]

These restrictions were put in place in the LPCC licensure act because the standard LPCC academic curriculum requires no training in couple or family work, and their licensure requirements demand no supervised experience with couples or families. These restrictions ensure that any LPCC working with a family will have appropriate preparation to do so.

It may be helpful to know that this law was not intended to ban normal non-therapeutic contacts between an LPCC and the parents of a child the LPCC is working with in therapy. Such contacts to simply *inform* the parents of what is happening in treatment or to schedule the next appointment do not reasonably seem like they would qualify as assessing or treating the family. Still, therapists of all kinds often want to do at least some family assessment to get a clear picture of the child's world.

So, while technically an LPCC can work with children individually without having completed the additional training and experience noted above, and can contact the family to keep them informed about what is happening in treatment, those LPCCs who do work with children will likely choose to complete the training and experience needed to enable them to work with the entire family.

---

[261] California Business & Professions Code section 4999.20

▶ Consent for treatment

> **Minors as young as 12 can independently consent for treatment.**
> Usually it is a parent or guardian who consents to their child's
> treatment. When custody is questionable, a qualifying relative
> can sign a "caregiver's authorization affidavit" asserting that they
> can give consent.

In most cases, you will be treating a minor under consent from
the minor's parent or guardian. If the minor has two legal parents,
typically, either parent may provide consent for the child's treatment.

When working with children whose parents are divorced or
were never married, matters of consent become more complicated.
Specific custody arrangements vary in how they handle children's
health care decision-making. Some custody agreements allow either
parent to provide consent, while others specify a particular parent as
having authority over health and medical care. In cases where a parent
is incapacitated or unavailable, consent becomes even more complex.

Fortunately, you do not need to get a DNA swab, a copy of the
divorce agreement, or other hard proof of guardian status from every
person who claims to be able to provide consent for a child's mental
health treatment. The law offers protection for clinicians who provide
treatment under a good-faith belief that the person who claimed to be
able to consent for a child's therapy is actually legally able to do so.[262]
For the therapist to get this protection, the person who brings a minor
in for therapy must be a relative (the term is broadly defined, and
includes stepfamily, half-siblings, cousins, grandparents, and so forth),
they must live in the same home as the child, and they must complete
a "Caregiver's authorization affidavit."[263] It is important that the
affidavit follow the very specific content and structure requirements
defined in law.[264] If you have the person providing consent for the
minor complete that affidavit, you are not required to do any

---

[262] California Family Code section 6550(c)

[263] I've provided a sample Caregiver's Authorization Affidavit for you at
www.bencaldwell.com/extras/caregivers-authorization-affidavit.pdf

[264] California Family Code section 6552

investigation of the accuracy of the claims of the person claiming to be a caregiver, and are not liable if the person was lying.[265]

Minors consenting on their own

Under legislation that took effect in 2011, **any minor age 12 or older can independently consent for their own psychotherapy**, as long as the therapist determines that the minor is mature enough to participate intelligently in therapy. In such cases, the minor is responsible for paying for therapy (the parents cannot be forced to pay for therapy for which they did not provide consent).[266]

As noted in the previous chapter, social work associates and trainees in all three professions need to proceed with some caution here. The letter of the law specifies only that minors can independently consent to treatment with licensees and with MFT and PCC interns,[267] leaving it unclear whether a minor could independently consent to being treated by a social work associate or a trainee from any profession.

When minors do consent for treatment on their own, it is important to remember that the therapist still must attempt to involve the parent or guardian unless the therapist can document why doing so would likely be detrimental (see "Involving family members" on the next page). It is also important to remember that parents do not have a right to access records for a minor seen under the minor's independent consent (see "Access to records" later in this chapter).

Emergencies

Parental consent is generally not required to treat a minor in life-threatening emergency situations, such as an immediate risk of serious physical harm to self or others.[268] However, this general rule comes with some meaningful cautions.

---

[265] California Family Code section 6552
[266] California Health & Safety Code section 124260(d)
[267] California Health & Safety Code section 124260(a)(2)
[268] California Business and Professions Code section 2395 exempts *physicians* from liability when acting in an emergency situation on patients of any age, though this law likely would not be considered to extend to master's-level

First of all, while there is some room in the law to provide emergency mental health care to a minor 12 or older in emergency situations (indeed, it even need not be an emergency, as you have read), it is not absolutely clear in the law when a child *under* 12 could be given emergency mental health treatment without parental consent. The law tends to defer to the judgment of professionals when acting on a good-faith belief that someone's life is in danger, and that would seem to reasonably include actively suicidal or homicidal clients. But if a minor under 12 is having some other kind of mental health emergency – a psychotic break, for example – and they do *not* appear to pose an immediate physical danger, it is less clear whether that minor could be given mental health treatment without parental consent under the emergency care rules.

In addition, the California Family Code statute that allows for emergency treatment of minors 12 and older without parental consent is written to apply to licensees and MFT and PCC interns only, and leaves out associate social workers and trainees from all three professions.[269] In *any* situation involving potential treatment of a minor without parental consent, trainees and social work associates should proceed with caution.

However, if a minor client's life is on the line, it would be sensible to place a higher priority on protecting that life than on technical concerns about legal compliance. As long as you provide competent care to the best of your ability and involve the parents and any other needed caregivers (and your supervisor, if you are not yet licensed) as quickly as possible, it would likely be challenging for a reasonable person to argue that you had made a mistake by intervening with a minor who presented immediate and life-threatening danger.

---

mental health professionals. California Family Code section 6924 allows for the mental health treatment of minors 12 and older without parental consent in emergency situations by master's level professionals, with the cautions noted above.

[269] California Family Code section 6924

▶ Involving family members and others

Working with any minor will mean doing at least some systemic conceptualization (that is, considering the family as a whole, and weighing the impact of other social systems) – children are greatly impacted by their family circumstances, and while their ability to change those circumstances grows with age, it often remains quite limited. Therapists may choose to involve family members, teachers, and other important people in a child's life in the therapy process in various ways.

When parents or guardians *must* be involved

Even when a minor consents for treatment on their own, a minor's parent or guardian must be brought into the therapy unless there is clear reason not to do so. When a minor consents independently for therapy, as the therapist, you must document (1) whether and when you attempted to contact the parent or guardian, and (2) whether each attempted contact was successful or unsuccessful. Alternatively, you may decide it would not be appropriate to contact the parent or guardian. In this case, you must document he reason why.[270]

Notably, these rules do not mean parents must be contacted before commencing treatment. The law specifically suggests that therapists make a determination about whether and how the parents should be involved *after* consulting with the minor.

If a parent or guardian provided consent for treatment on a child's behalf, the level of involvement of the parents in ongoing treatment becomes a clinical decision. Unless there is a specific, documented reason not to involve the parents in therapy, it would be highly unusual for a therapist to work with a child without meeting with the parents at some point, typically early in the treatment process. Failing to do so could be considered a violation of the standard of care, because the overwhelming majority of therapists would meet with the parents. How often the parents are met with and how much information is shared with them are up to the clinical

---

[270] California Health & Safety Code section 124260(c)

judgment of the therapist, but typically a therapist would meet with the parents of younger children more often, and the parents of older children less often. Regardless of the child's age, parents should be included in treatment in some way unless there is good reason not to.

Involving other important adults

In assessing a child's behavior and their progress in therapy, it can be useful to discuss the minor and their treatment with other adults. For example, teachers can be very helpful in determining whether a minor's troubling behavior is limited to the home, or occurring at school as well.

In order to make contact with any other important adults in a child's life, and share information with them about the minor's treatment, you must have a signed Release of Information that allows you to disclose information that would normally be confidential. If the minor consented for therapy on their own, the minor must be the one to authorize this release. If a parent or guardian consented for the minor's treatment, the parent or guardian must be the one to sign the release.[271]

Minors hold their own privilege

Recall from our discussion in Chapter 5 (Confidentiality, Privilege, and Exceptions) that under California law, minors typically hold their own privilege.[272] However, minors generally cannot make legal decisions, so minors are only allowed to waive privilege in some instances. Ultimately, if a minor wishes to waive privilege, the decision will be up to a judge, who will weigh the minor's age and maturity among other factors.

---

[271] California Welfare and Institutions Code section 5328, California Civil Code sections 56.10 and 56.11
[272] California Welfare and Institutions Code section 317(f)

▶ Access to records

If a minor has consented to services on their own, the minor has a right to access their own records. If the minor's parent or guardian provided consent for the minor's treatment, the parent or guardian has a right to access those records.[273] In either case, the therapist has some latitude to refuse to release treatment records if the therapist can document that doing so would likely be harmful to the minor or to the therapy process. (The therapist must note the date of the request and the specific description of the negative consequences the therapist believes would occur for the minor if the records were released.[274]) If there is no such likely harm from releasing the records, the therapist must allow records to be inspected within five working days of a request, or provide photocopies of the records within 15 days of receiving a request. Requests to inspect or receive copies of records must be made in writing.[275]

Records from individual therapy with a minor

When parents consent to the treatment of their children, the parents typically have a legal right to access the treatment records for the child. When a minor consents to treatment on their own, the parents do NOT have a right to the minor's treatment records. Only the minor themselves can authorize the release of their own records.[276]

Records from family therapy involving a minor

If you have been working with a minor as part of family therapy, releasing records to any family member requires consent from *all* family members who provided consent for treatment originally. (After all, if you are keeping one treatment record for the family, it is impossible to release one person's records without releasing the records of others.) Typically this means all family members over the

---

[273] California Health and Safety Code section 123110(a)
[274] California Health and Safety Code section 123115(a) and (b)
[275] California Health and Safety Code section 123110(a) and (b)
[276] California Health and Safety Code section 123110(a)

age of 18, as parents usually provide consent on behalf of minors in family therapy contexts.[277]

---

[277] California Civil Code section 5610

▶ Reporting suspected child abuse

All mental health professionals in California are categorized as mandated reporters for known or suspected child abuse.[278] However, this only applies when you are acting in your professional capacity. When you are outside of your therapist role, you are not a mandated reporter. For example, you are not required by law to report a mother you observe physically abusing her child in a grocery store.[279] Of course, even when you are outside of your mandated-reporter role, you are still *allowed* to make a report of suspected child abuse – you just are not required to do so.[280]

What is reportable

The following types of suspected child abuse **must** be reported:

- **Physical abuse**
- **Sexual abuse**
- **Willful harm or endangerment**
- **Neglect**
- **Abuse in out-of-home care**

In addition, **emotional abuse operates under a permissive reporting standard**, which means that mandated reporters may report the emotional abuse of a child but are not required to do so by law.[281] Children witnessing domestic violence are often reported as victims of emotional abuse.

The following are brief descriptions of what qualifies as abuse under each category. More detailed descriptions can be found in a number of documents available online.[282] While this guide is focused

---

[278] California Penal Code section 11165.7(a)(21)
[279] California Penal Code section 11166
[280] California Penal Code section 11166(g)
[281] California Penal Code section 11166.05
[282] Though it isn't specifically tailored to California law, McCoy and Keen's *Child Abuse and Neglect* differentiates categories of abuse well.

---

on the legal, rather than the clinical, aspects of reporting child abuse, there are a number of good articles and textbooks on the clinical assessment and potential indicators of child abuse.[283]

Physical abuse (unlawful corporal punishment)

Physical abuse is defined in the law as any situation where any person **willfully causes an injury to a child** or engages in cruel or inhuman corporal punishment. In practice, it can be thought of like this: If a parent disciplines their child with an open hand in a way that does not leave a bruise or injury, it is likely not abusive. If the punishment does leave an injury on the child, it is abusive.

There are a number of specific exceptions to the standards for physical abuse. Police officers operating in the normal scope of their duties are not considered to be abusing children when they use physical force to control a situation. Similarly, school employees are not considered abusive when they use physical force to control a disturbance or to remove weapons or other dangerous objects from a child's control.[284] Finally, children fighting by mutual consent (as in a common schoolyard fight) are not considered to be abusing each other.[285]

Sexual abuse

California law defines two types of child sexual abuse. "Sexual assault" includes incest, oral sex, anal sex (sodomy), sexual penetration, lewd and lascivious acts, child molestation, and *some forms of* statutory rape. Of these, oral and anal sex and object penetration are fairly self-explanatory. Any penetration of the mouth or anal opening by the penis are considered oral or anal sex, even if they do not lead to orgasm.[286] Similarly, any penetration of the

---

[283] The U.S. Department of Health and Human Services' Child Welfare Information Gateway includes many resources on recognizing and responding to different kinds of abuse and neglect. Start with *Recognizing Child Abuse and Neglect: Signs and Symptoms*, which is a free factsheet.
[284] California Penal Code section 11165.4
[285] California Penal Code section 11165.6
[286] California Penal Code section 11165.1(b)

genitals or anal opening of another person using an object (including body parts) is considered to be abusive.

In addition to the kinds of behaviors that you would expect to be included in sexual assault (fondling, masturbating an another's presence, etc.) "lewd and lascivious acts" and "child molestation" broaden the scope of sexually abusive behavior to include such acts as videotaping children undressing, soliciting prostitution from a minor, flashing, and a variety of other behaviors.[287]

The other type of child sexual abuse is "sexual exploitation." It occurs when parents or other adults encourage a child to participate in sexually explicit acts, performances, or depictions. A caregiver is committing sexual exploitation if they allow such acts to take place, even if they do not play an active role in them.[288]

When adolescents of similar chronological and maturational age are engaging in heterosexual, vaginal intercourse, it may or may not qualify as sexual abuse under California's reporting laws. See "Reporting consensual sexual activity" on the next page.

Willful harm or endangerment

This category is not particularly defined in law. Any person causing a child **"unjustifiable physical pain or mental suffering,"** or any caregiver allowing it to happen, is committing this form of abuse.[289]

Neglect

A child is the victim of neglect if the person responsible for their welfare fails to provide adequate food, clothing, shelter, medical care, or supervision. Neglect is the only category of abuse that can occur by omission (the *failure* to do something). It is reportable even if it takes place by accident. It is important to understand that a child need not have suffered actual harm before a report of neglect can be made.[290]

---

[287] California Penal Code sections 288, 647.6, and 11165.1(a) and (b)
[288] California Penal Code section 11165.1(c)
[289] California Penal Code section 11165.3
[290] California Penal Code section 11165.2

The law allows parents to make "informed and appropriate" decisions regarding medical care on the child's behalf. These may include the refusal of medical treatment or a choice to participate in spiritual treatment. These decisions, on their own, are not considered neglect.[291]

Abuse in out-of-home care

The law specifically lists abuse in out-of-home care (such as a day care) as its own category for reporting purposes. It is something of a catch-all category for **physical injury or death that occurs to minors in child-care or school settings.**[292]

Emotional abuse

If a child is suffering "serious emotional damage" or is at substantial risk of suffering such damage, a therapist is allowed to make a report of suspected child abuse. However, **the emotional abuse category is <u>not</u> a mandated report.** It is a *permissive* report, meaning that you can make a report, and are protected from lawsuits if you do. However, there is no penalty for failing to report.[293]

The emotional abuse standard requires that there be some behavioral evidence of the emotional harm the child is suffering or at risk of suffering. This can include severe anxiety, depression, withdrawal, or aggression (including aggression toward self).

Reporting consensual sexual activity

When specifically considering heterosexual, vaginal intercourse, it is important to bear in mind that behavior that is *illegal* is not necessarily *abusive*. When a 19-year-old engages in sexual intercourse with a 16-year-old, the 19-year-old is committing statutory rape.[294] However, this combination of ages does not qualify as child

---

[291] California Penal Code section 11165.2(b)
[292] California Penal Code section 11165.5
[293] California Penal Code section 11166.05
[294] California Penal Code section 261.5

abuse under the law. The child abuse standards are specific in only including some categories of unlawful sexual intercourse as reportable:

Table 6.1: Is consensual heterosexual intercourse involving minors reportable?[295]

Client age	Partner age			
	Under 14	14-15	16-20	21 or over
Under 14	No*	Yes - Report	Yes - Report	Yes - Report
14-15	Yes - Report	No*	No*	Yes - Report
16-20	Yes - Report	No*	No*	No*
21 or over	Yes - Report	Yes - Report	No*	No*

* - In some instances, even when partners are of similar age their sexual activity can be considered coerced (and thus reportable). For example, if one partner was drunk, or if one partner was threatened or intimidated into the act, the sexual activity may be reportable even if the minor tells you they gave consent.

Other forms of sexual activity, including oral sex, anal sex, and object penetration for sexual purposes (including any part of the body other than a penis) are always considered child abuse under the law if a minor is involved.[296] However, this would appear to create different standards for reporting sexual activity of heterosexual adolescents as opposed to gay and lesbian adolescents. In April of 2013, the Department of Consumer Affairs (which oversees the BBS) issued a memo interpreting current law as allowing therapists to use their discretion in determining whether to report such acts if the acts were consensual and within acceptable age ranges as defined in the chart above.[297] Since this memo is simply one interpretation of the law, and the underlying statute is still in place, some attorneys are continuing to advise therapists that the safest route is to follow the statute.

---

[295] Adapted from *Understanding Confidentiality and Minor Consent in California*, which includes full legal referencing. Sources include California Penal Code sections 261, 261.5(d), and 11165.1
[296] California Penal Code section 11165.1(b)
[297] Dobbs, D. R. (2013). *Evaluation of CANRA reform proposal related to reporting of consensual sex between minors.* Memo dated April 11, 2013.

Sexting and other digital media

Under a change law that took effect January 1, 2015, mandated reporters of child abuse must report any time they have reasonable suspicion that someone knowingly "downloads [...] streams, or otherwise accesses through any electronic or digital media" any images or videos that involve minors engaging in "an act of obscene sexual conduct."[298]

While the aims of this bill were good – CANRA was written before the development of the Internet, and the legislature wanted to clarify that digital distribution of child pornography qualifies as child abuse in the same way that print distribution of child pornography does – the language of this change has come to be seen by many as problematic. In a technical sense, minors who are voluntarily "sexting" each other sexual images of themselves could be seen as committing child abuse based on this language. Even more troubling, those who *download* the images are considered to be abusers; in other words, both the sender and recipient of a sext can be considered to have committed a crime. This language may be further amended so that it has its intended effect of capturing those who distribute child porn online, without capturing those who do not reasonably fit the definition of a child abuser.

"Reasonable suspicion"

Under state law, if you are a mental health professional and develop a "reasonable suspicion" that child abuse has taken place, it must be reported. Often therapists will ask what exactly "reasonable suspicion" means: Do you need to have seen physical evidence? Do you need to be absolutely sure?

The law offers a definition of reasonable suspicion:

> For purposes of this article, "reasonable suspicion" means that it is objectively reasonable for a person to entertain a suspicion, based upon facts that could cause a reasonable person in a like position, drawing, when appropriate, on his or her training and experience, to suspect child abuse or neglect.

---

[298] California Penal Code section 11165.3(c)(3)

> "Reasonable suspicion" does not require certainty
> that child abuse or neglect has occurred nor does it
> require a specific medical indication of child abuse
> or neglect; any "reasonable suspicion" is
> sufficient.[299]

This description answers both of the questions above, and also provides a clear avenue therapists can use to check and see whether their suspicion level meets the "reasonable suspicion" standard: Consult. Without revealing identifying information about the specific clients, **consulting with colleagues and supervisors you know and trust will help determine whether a report is appropriate.**

It is important to note that the law does not require therapists to take on the role of investigating potential child abuse. **You are not an investigator.** Reporting should be determined based on information gained in the normal process of therapy – you do not need to gather information you would not normally gather in order to determine whether a report should be made.[300]

What if you're wrong?

The law is designed to encourage therapists to err on the side of reporting. From the perspective of protecting vulnerable children, it is better for the state to receive suspected child abuse reports that cannot be verified than it is for the state to *not* receive reports that *would* turn out to be verifiable.

A therapist is protected from any civil or criminal liability for making a good-faith report of suspected child abuse, even if investigators are unable to substantiate the report.[301]

---

[299] California Penal Code section 11166(a)(1)
[300] *People v. Stockton Pregnancy Control Medical Clinic*, 203 Cal. App. 3d 225, 1988
[301] California Penal Code section 11172

Filing a report

Once you have developed reasonable suspicion that abuse has taken place, it must be reported to a local child welfare agency immediately. Such agencies include local police or sheriff's departments, the county welfare department, or in some locations, the county's probation office. While your county will have specific procedures in regard to who ultimately investigates suspected child abuse, under the law you are allowed to make your report to any agency authorized to receive such reports.[302] They must take your report or immediately transfer your call to someone who can, and it is then up to them to forward the report appropriately.

> **Suspected child abuse must be reported by phone immediately.** This must be followed up with a written report within 36 hours.

The phone report must be followed up with a written report within 36 hours. There are no exceptions to these timeframes for weekends or holidays. When making the initial phone report, be sure to ask where the written report is to be sent, and how they prefer to receive it (fax or mail). Most agencies will prefer to receive the report by fax, so that they will have it more immediately.

The written report form can be found online.[303] You should file the report even if you do not have all of the information it requests.[304]

Penalties for failing to make a mandated report

A therapist who fails to report known or reasonably suspected abuse can be sentenced to up to six months in jail, a $1,000 fine, or both.[305] The penalties are greater if the abuse results in death or severe injury.[306] Covering up a failure to report is considered a continuing offense until the time it is discovered, effectively meaning that a

---

[302] California Penal Code section 11165.9
[303] http://oag.ca.gov/childabuse/forms (scroll to "Suspected Child Abuse Report Form")
[304] California Penal Code section 11167(a)
[305] California Penal Code section 11166(c)
[306] California Penal Code section 11166.01

therapist can be punished for covering up a failure to report even if it is not discovered for many years.

Of greater concern than criminal penalties and lawsuits should be the human consequences of failing to report child abuse. Any time a mandated reporter knows of or reasonably suspects abuse and does nothing, that inaction enables the abuser to continue abusing children, while their victims go without protection or resources.

Abuse that occurred out of state

Abuse that occurred out of state is still reportable. It should be reported to your local child welfare agency. It is then up to them to determine whether and how to forward the information to the place where the abuse happened.

Reporting when the abuser or victim has died

The law specifically requires reporting when the victim has died,[307] and does not make any exceptions to reporting for instances when the abuser has died. Even in these cases, there still is a compelling state interest in knowing about and investigating the abuse. There may be other victims in need of assistance, and there may have been others involved in the abuse.

Reporting when the abuser has moved away or no longer has access to children

The above are two excuses I commonly hear therapists give for not reporting suspected child abuse. However, **the law does not make an exception for either of these excuses**, and it makes sense that there would be no such exception. Abusers should not be able to escape responsibility for their actions simply by moving to a new place. Someone who does not have access to children now (for example, if they are incarcerated) may regain access to children in the future, and they still should be held responsible for any past abusive

---

[307] California Penal Code section 11166.2

acts. In either instance, there may be additional victims of abuse who could benefit from resources being made available to them.

Reporting when the victim is now an adult

California law requires reporting when a therapist has knowledge of or witnesses *a child* who is the victim of suspected abuse. CAMFT has construed this to mean that therapists do not report when an adult client reveals they were abused as a child.[308] Of course, the victim can still be encouraged to report the abuse on their own to law enforcement.

---

[308] Benitez, B. R. (1999 November/December). Reporting consensual sexual activity involving minors. *The Therapist.*

7

Working with Elders and Dependent Adults

Minors are not the only vulnerable population in the state. Elders and dependent adults are also considered to be at risk for abuse and neglect, and so the state requires health care providers to report known or suspected instances of elder and dependent adult abuse. As some elder and dependent adults lose their capacity for effective self-care, they may go through a court process that allows others to take on their legal rights and responsibilities.

▶ Key definitions

Knowing the specific meanings of the terms "elder" and "dependent adult" is essential to appropriate abuse reporting. California's definitions of these terms differ from those of many other states.

Elder

Under California law, an "elder" is anyone age 65 or older *residing in the state of California*.[309] That last part is important – a 67-year-old who lives out of state and is simply in California on vacation is *not* an elder under the law. If such a person were to suffer abuse while in the state, a therapist is *not* required to report that abuse. In fact, such a report could be considered a breach of confidentiality.

So what does it mean, exactly, to reside here? California tax law defines a resident as anyone in the state "for other than a temporary or transitory purpose." Those who live in California and are outside of the state temporarily are also considered residents for tax purposes.[310] Ultimately, determining residency can be a surprisingly complex factual question; if you have a client whose residency status you are not sure of, you may want to consult with an attorney.

Dependent Adult

Any California resident (the same residency requirement applies here as in the above definition of "elder") who is age 18-64 and cannot carry out their normal activities or protect their own rights because of physical or mental health issues is a "dependent adult" in the eyes of the state. This includes the physically or developmentally disabled, and those whose physical or mental abilities have diminished with age. It also includes anyone who has been admitted as an inpatient to a hospital or other 24-hour health care facility.[311]

---

[309] California Welfare and Institutions Code section 15610.27
[310] California Revenue and Taxation Code section 17014; California Code of Regulations title 18 section 17014
[311] California Welfare and Institutions Code section 15610.23

It is important to note that a person does not need to have had their legal rights restricted (under conservatorship, for example) to be considered a dependent adult. By including those not able to carry out their normal activities, the definition is fairly broad. It is also common for people to fit the definition only temporarily, and then to recover from whatever condition had kept them from normal activities. One does not need to be permanently disabled to be a dependent adult.

▸ Reporting elder and dependent adult abuse

> **The rules and process for reporting elder and dependent adult abuse changed significantly in 2012.** Recognized types of abuse and rules for reporting differ in important ways from reportable child abuse.

The reporting guidelines for elder and dependent adult abuse changed significantly in 2012. While the reportable categories of abuse stayed the same as they have been, the reporting process changed significantly. Now, instead of a single rule for how quickly a report must be made and to whom it must be made, there are five different sets of standards, based on a number of factors surrounding the suspected abuse.

What is reportable

California law recognizes seven types of elder or dependent adult abuse that, if reasonably suspected by a therapist, must be reported. As with children, it is also allowed, but not required, to report emotional abuse. Unlike the laws for children, mandated **reporters also have a permissive standard for reporting *any* other form of elder or dependent adult abuse not specified here;** they may make a report if they choose to, but are not required to.[312]

Physical abuse

Physical abuse includes physical attacks (assault, battery, and the like), unreasonable physical restraint, and depriving a person of food or water. Various forms of sexual abuse are also included in the definition of physical abuse.[313]

---

[312] California Welfare and Institutions Code section 15630(c)(1)
[313] California Welfare and Institutions Code section 15610.63

One does not have to have been assaulted to have been physically abused, however. Physical restraints, chemical restraints, and psychotropic drugs are all abusive if used for punishment or for any reason not authorized by a physician. This is one reason why you as a therapist do not need to see a physical injury in order to reasonably suspect abuse has taken place: Not all kinds of abuse, and even not all kinds of physical abuse, leave visible marks.

Abandonment

Caretakers for elder and dependent adults willingly take on responsibility for those adults' well-being. If a caretaker deserts their patient or gives up on their responsibilities when a reasonable person would not have done so, this is considered abandonment.[314]

Abduction

Under the abuse reporting statutes, for abduction to have occurred, the elder or dependent adult must have been *taken outside the state of California or prevented from returning* to the state, and they must not have the ability to consent to this.[315] If an elder or dependent adult is moved against their will within the state, this would not appear to qualify as abduction for the purposes of abuse reporting. However, it may fall within the definition of isolation.

Isolation

No elder or dependent adult should be needlessly kept from contact with their loved ones. Any attempts to prevent normal contact are considered isolation and are reportable as abuse. Examples in the law include preventing an elder or dependent adult from receiving their mail or telephone calls, telling callers or visitors that the person is not present or does not want to visit with them (when that isn't true), and physically restraining someone from seeing visitors.[316]

---

[314] California Welfare and Institutions Code section 15610.05
[315] California Welfare and Institutions Code section 15610.06
[316] California Welfare and Institutions Code section 15610.43

Financial abuse

Unlike minors, who rarely have significant financial resources of their own, elder and dependent adults are vulnerable to having their money or other resources taken. California law protects elders and dependent adults from such abuse. Note that financial abuse can occur even when the victim knowingly gave their money or property to another person, if that other person has an "unfair advantage" (that actually is language used in the law)[317] over the victim by virtue of their position of trust or authority or because of the victim's needs, distress, or weakness of mind.

As you can see, the law here is purposefully broad. Of course, elders and dependent adults still have control over their money and property, unless they have had their legal rights restricted for some reason. They can choose to give their money or possessions away. It is only financial abuse if the recipient took the gift "for wrongful use or with intent to defraud," or if they knew or should have known that taking the gift would be harmful to the elder or dependent adult.

Neglect

Neglect can be difficult to assess, particularly when the concern is that an elder is neglecting their own care. For this reason, the law defines neglect in some detail. There are four key areas: Hygiene, medical care, health and safety hazards, and malnutrition/dehydration.[318] Any person responsible for the care of an elder who is not ensuring that these four areas are being appropriately addressed can be reported for neglect.[319]

It is not only caregivers who may neglect an elder or dependent adult. Elder or dependent adults can be reported for neglecting themselves.[320] The intent of the law when it comes to self-neglect is not to punish those who are unable to adequately care for themselves, but rather, to ensure that they are provided with a level of care appropriate to their needs.

---

[317] California Civil Code section 1575
[318] California Welfare and Institutions Code section 15610.57(b)
[319] California Welfare and Institutions Code section 15610.57(a)
[320] California Welfare and Institutions Code section 15610.57(a)(2)

Reasonable suspicion

As is the case with child abuse reporting, the "reasonable suspicion" standard for reporting asks you whether "a reasonable person in a like position, drawing when appropriate upon his or her training and experience" would suspect abuse to have taken place.[321] This underscores the importance of consulting with colleagues and supervisors if you are not sure whether a report is warranted.

One key difference from the child abuse reporting standards, though, occurs when an elder or dependent adult tells you directly that they are the victim of abuse. With a minor, you would use your professional judgment to determine whether you reasonably believe that report. With an elder or dependent adult, the law is specific that you *must* report any instance of abuse that an elder or dependent adult tells you about directly[322] – *even if you do not believe them* – unless *all three* of the following are true: (1) the client has been diagnosed with a mental illness or dementia (or is under a conservatorship for that reason), (2) you reasonably believe the abuse did not happen, and (3) you are aware of no evidence that would support the claim of abuse.[323]

Filing a report

This is where things can get a little complicated. Two laws passed in 2012 have greatly altered the elder and dependent adult abuse reporting timelines and destinations. Thankfully, these changes only apply to abuse that occurs in a long-term care facility.

Known or suspected instances of elder and dependent adult abuse *that occurred outside of a long-term care facility* must be reported by phone or Internet immediately, and in writing within two working days, to law enforcement or your local adult protective services agency.[324] If the initial report was filed by Internet, as is now possible in some counties, a separate written follow-up is not necessary.

---

[321] California Welfare and Institutions Code section 15610.65
[322] California Welfare and Institutions Code section 15630(b)(1)
[323] California Welfare and Institutions Code section 15630(b)(3)
[324] California Welfare and Institutions Code section 15630(b)(1)

For abuse that takes place *inside* a long-term care facility, how long you have to file the written report and who that report goes to will vary based on the circumstances of the case. In some cases, as many as three separate written reports must be filed within a specific timeframe. To see where these reports must go, and how long you have to file them, see "Decision tree for reporting elder and dependent adult abuse" on the next page.

Ombudspersons

If you are examining the reporting requirements for suspected abuse that occurs in long-term care, you may be wondering, *What exactly is an ombudsperson?* Each county has a long-term care ombudsperson, and there is a directory of them on the web site of the state's Department of Aging.[325]

Long-term care ombudspersons serve two purposes: (1) They receive and work to resolve complaints from individual long-term care residents, and (2) They work with the state Department of Aging and with other local and state officials to develop policies and practices that will best serve the larger long-term care population.[326] In both cases, ombudspersons exist to support and advocate for the interests of residents.

---

[325] www.aging.ca.gov/programs/LTCOP/Contacts/
[326] California Department of Aging: Long Term Care Ombudsman Program

▶ Decision tree for reporting suspected elder or dependent adult abuse

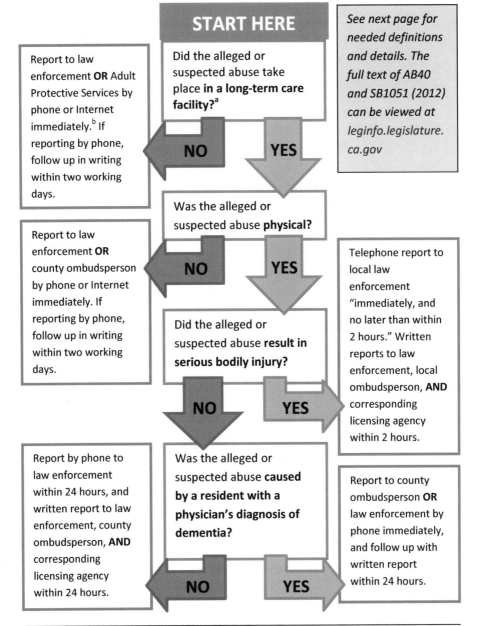

START HERE

Did the alleged or suspected abuse take place **in a long-term care facility?**[a]

See next page for needed definitions and details. The full text of AB40 and SB1051 (2012) can be viewed at leginfo.legislature.ca.gov

NO → Report to law enforcement **OR** Adult Protective Services by phone or Internet immediately.[b] If reporting by phone, follow up in writing within two working days.

YES ↓

Was the alleged or suspected abuse **physical?**

NO → Report to law enforcement **OR** county ombudsperson by phone or Internet immediately. If reporting by phone, follow up in writing within two working days.

YES ↓

Did the alleged or suspected abuse **result in serious bodily injury?**

YES → Telephone report to local law enforcement "immediately, and no later than within 2 hours." Written reports to law enforcement, local ombudsperson, **AND** corresponding licensing agency within 2 hours.

NO ↓

Was the alleged or suspected abuse **caused by a resident with a physician's diagnosis of dementia?**

YES → Report to county ombudsperson **OR** law enforcement by phone immediately, and follow up with written report within 24 hours.

NO → Report by phone to law enforcement within 24 hours, and written report to law enforcement, county ombudsperson, **AND** corresponding licensing agency within 24 hours.

Definitions and clarifications

SB1051 was signed into law by Governor Jerry Brown and took effect immediately; AB40 was also signed and made additional changes effective January 1, 2013.

a – Other than a state mental hospital or state developmental center. If the suspected or alleged abuse occurred in a state mental hospital or a state developmental center, the report shall be made to designated investigators of the State Department of State Hospitals or the State Department of Developmental Services, or to the local law enforcement agency (Welfare & Institutions Code 15630(b)(1)(E)).

b – Unless otherwise specified, "immediately" means "immediately or as soon as practicably possible" (WIC 15630(b)(1) and (b)(1)(A)(iii)).

"Serious bodily injury" = "an injury involving extreme physical pain, substantial risk of death, or protracted loss or impairment of function of a bodily member, organ, or of mental faculty, or requiring medical intervention, including, but not limited to, hospitalization, surgery, or physical rehabilitation" (WIC 15610.67).

Elder abuse reporting form and instructions

www.dss.cahwnet.gov/Forms/English/SOC341.pdf

Find your local ombudsperson

www.aging.ca.gov/programs/LTCOP/Contacts/

View the full text of AB40 & SB1051 (2012)

leginfo.legislature.ca.gov/faces/billNavClient.xhtml?bill_id=201120120AB40
leginfo.legislature.ca.gov/faces/billNavClient.xhtml?bill_id=201120120SB1051

▶ Conservatorship and legal standing

Elders and dependent adults may have someone else take responsibility for their health care or finances through the process of conservatorship. Less drastic measures are preferred when possible.

One of the biggest challenges for elders and dependent adults, as well as their families, is managing their legal rights and responsibilities. Elders and dependent adults who lack the ability to care for themselves or make sound decisions may have their legal rights scaled back by a court in a process known as conservatorship.[327]

In a conservatorship, a court appoints someone (the conservator) to care for the adult who is unable to care for themselves or manage their own money (the conservatee). California has two types of conservatorships: Probate conservatorships and Lanterman-Petris-Short (LPS) conservatorships.

Probate conservatorships are much more commonly used. In probate conservatorships, the conservator may be responsible for the conservatee (including their living arrangements, health care, and general well-being), the conservatee's finances (including paying bills, responsibly investing, and budgeting), or both, depending on the conservatee's needs. A spouse, relative, other interested party, or even the person needing conservatorship can file a request for conservatorship with the court.

LPS conservatorships are much more rare, and are only used when adults have serious mental health problems that require extensive care and they are unable or unwilling to receive that care. A family member or caregiver cannot apply for this kind of conservatorship on their own; the process must be started by a local government agency. These conservatorships only apply for one year,

---

[327] The information in this section is drawn from the California Courts Conservatorship page, which offers a wealth of additional resources for anyone considering asking the court to appoint a conservator for themselves or a loved one. www.courts.ca.gov/selfhelp-conservatorship.htm

and only can be used when someone is gravely disabled due to mental illness.

In either instance, because a conservatorship by definition involves taking some of the adult's legal rights away, courts will prefer less-intrusive means of ensuring that the adult is properly cared for if at all possible. Someone who is initially unwilling to appropriately care for themselves may change their mind when faced with the possibility of being placed in conservatorship. For financial issues, courts may prefer that the client voluntarily set up a power of attorney arrangement, giving a trusted person control over financial decisions, rather than using the more-intrusive conservatorship route.

8

Advertising

Once someone has met the standards necessary to call themselves a "Professional Clinical Counselor," a "Clinical Social Worker," or a "Marriage and Family Therapist," the ability to advertise those services is good for everyone: It helps therapists build their preferred clientele (ultimately allowing them to make a living), helps prospective clients find the therapist who is the best fit for their needs, and helps raise broader public awareness about available mental health services. However, such advertising must protect and preserve the public trust placed in psychotherapists. This can be a challenging balance.

▶ Overarching guidelines

While California law can be achingly complex and highly specific, much of the law on advertising comes down to two simple ideas:

1. **Be truthful and honest in how you represent yourself to the public.**
2. **Include required disclosures, such as your licensure status, in all advertising.**

Much of this chapter focuses on the specific words and titles you are allowed or not allowed to use, and when their usage is appropriate. That's the letter of the law. California law is also written in such a way as to require adherence to its spirit. So you should not try to find ways to be *technically* compliant that would still violate either of the two principles above.

For example, if you are a social work associate, and you include this fact on your business cards in type so small that most people would need a magnifying glass to read it, you couldn't argue that you had followed the law; your card could still be seen as misleading. The BBS defines any misrepresentation of *any* of the following to be unprofessional conduct:[328]

- The type of a license or registration held
- The status of a license or registration held
- Education
- Professional qualifications
- Professional affiliations

The term "misrepresentation" does not simply mean lying or making false statements. It would also apply to anything you produce that a reasonable person would find misleading.

Through a regulatory change that took place in 2013, the BBS gained what is commonly called cite-and-fine authority over advertising. While of course they could pursue an action against your

---

[328] California Business and Professions Code section 4982(f)

license or registration if your advertising qualifies as false or misleading, that is a time-consuming and expensive process (see Chapter 3). It is much faster for the BBS to simply issue a cease-and-desist order and require you to pay a fine if they find your advertising to be problematic, and they can now do so.[329]

As you will see in this chapter, if your ads are truthful and honest, if they include your required disclosures in obvious places, and if you use good judgment in deciding what content to include in your ads, you should be in safe territory.

---

[329] California Code of Regulations title 16 section 1811(e)

▶ Who is allowed to advertise

> **Licensees, MFT interns, CSW associates, and PCC interns can advertise. Trainees can't advertise their own services,** but agencies can advertise services provided by trainees.

Any licensed mental health professional can advertise their services. Interns and associates are also specifically allowed to advertise,[330] though any advertisement of prelicensees' services must include additional disclosures (see "Advertisements for interns, associates, and trainees" later in this chapter).

Trainees cannot advertise on their own. However, it is common for the agencies and other workplaces where trainees work to advertise services provided by trainees. Such ads also require additional disclosures.

If you are working for an agency, group practice, or other organization, you should pay close attention to any ads that the organization produces that discuss you or your services. Even when you are not the person doing the advertising, you have a responsibility to ensure that any advertisements distributed on your behalf are not false or misleading. In other words, **you may be held responsible for any advertising that is *about* you, even if you yourself did not produce the ad.**

---

[330] California Code of Regulations title 16 section 1811(c)(d)(e)

▶ What qualifies as an advertisement

> **The definition of an advertisement is purposefully broad.** It includes basically any way that you communicate to the public about your services.

The definition of an advertisement in California law is very broad. Essentially, **any "public communication" about your services – in speech, in print, or in any other media, including the Internet – qualifies as an advertisement.** The only exceptions are signs posted in religious buildings and notices in bulletins mailed to religious congregations.[331]

The phrase "about your services" is important there. Just because you are a therapist does not mean that anything you say to anyone is an advertisement. However, it does mean that any time your professional role or professional services are mentioned in a venue that could lead someone to come to your practice, you are obligated to make sure the discussion of your services is truthful and accurate, and that you make the disclosures required in the law.

That means that all of the following, depending on their specific content, can qualify as advertisements:

- Business cards
- Flyers, postcards, and brochures
- Therapist directories
- Email
- Web sites
- Blogs
- Facebook pages
- Tweets
- Google ads

We will discuss each in more detail. With all of them, the law does not specify how big the type has to be for your required

---

[331] California Business and Professions Code sections 4980.03(e), 4989.49, 4992.2, and 4999.12(j)

disclosures, nor does it specify where those disclosures need to be (the front of a business card as opposed to the back, for example). However, the law specifically prohibits advertising that is misleading about one's licensure or registration status, and it stands to reason that **making your disclosures too small or too hard to find could be considered misleading**, even if you have included all of the required text.

Business cards

Business cards are among the most common tools therapists use to promote their practices, and to provide convenient contact information to colleagues and prospective clients alike. Because they are made to be widely distributed, business cards easily meet the definition of an advertisement if they include any mention of your professional role or services.

Flyers, postcards, and brochures

Printed materials like flyers, postcards, and brochures are commonly used to offer information about a therapist's practice, and all clearly fall within the definition of advertising.

Therapist directories

Whether in print or online, therapist directories (such as those at GoodTherapy.org and PsychologyToday.com) qualify as advertisements. In some cases, directories may list you without any knowledge or action on your part. While it is not your job to police the Internet, if you do come across information about you that is inaccurate, you should attempt to correct it.

Email

Email occupies something of a gray area. A private message to individuals with whom you have a prior relationship seems unlikely to be considered "public communication." However, any email you send can be forwarded to people you do not know, so even private discussions of your practice should be approached with caution. Using email to promote your practice (through an e-newsletter, for example) would more clearly be public communication, and thus count as an ad.

Therapists who regularly include their title, or any mention of services offered, in their email signatures may be engaging in "public communication" under the definition in the law. It would seem safest to consider those signatures to be advertising and include all required disclosures.

CAMFT has noted a trend of prelicensed therapists using license titles or abbreviations in their email addresses.[332] This can be considered misleading and should be avoided. For example, if you are a registered MFT intern (or anything other than a licensed MFT), you should not use an email address that includes the initials MFT.

Web sites

If you advertise your practice through a web site, bear in mind that through search engines or even printouts of your site, someone may land on a specific page within your site without ever seeing your home page or a page with your biographical information. For this reason, therapists commonly **consider each individual page on a web site to be an advertisement.** They then include the required disclosures on each and every page of the site.

As is the case with choosing email addresses, you should choose your web domain name carefully to avoid misleading visitors. If you are not yet licensed, advertising your practice with a web domain like "JaneDoeMFT.com" or "JaneDoeClinicalCounselor.com" could be considered misleading. Only include a professional title or abbreviation in your domain name if you are qualified to use that title or abbreviation.

Several requirements specific to counselors' use of web sites were added to the ACA Code of Ethics in 2014. These requirements include having links to relevant licensure and certification boards (in California, presumably that would mean including a link to the BBS web site at www.bbs.ca.gov), regularly ensuring that all the links on your site are working properly and are professionally appropriate, and providing accessibility to persons with disabilities. When feasible,

---

[332] Tran-Lien, A. (2012). Ten advertising mistakes made by therapists. *The Therapist*, March/April 2012.

counselors should also provide translation capacities for clients who speak a different language.[333] On the last point, web site translations can be fairly easily offered by including a service like Google Translate on your site; even the BBS itself does so. Of course, such translations are likely to be imperfect, a fact that you may want to ensure that your web site visitors know.

Blogs

Blog posts may or may not be considered advertising, depending on their content. A post that is informational in nature (for example, discussion of a recent scientific study that has been in the news) and makes no mention of your professional services seems unlikely to be considered an advertisement for those services. However, if you so much as suggest that you do therapy – through your title, through mentioning that you see clients, or through any other means – you are advertising.

I struggled with this very issue in my own online writing. I maintain a blog on policy, research, and professional issues in the field of family therapy at www.PsychotherapyNotes.com. Even though most posts do not mention my practice, I was reticent to take any chances. That's why each and every blog entry features my licensure information on the right-hand side of the page. That doesn't mean you have to do the same thing; it just means I chose to err on the side of caution.

Facebook

Facebook certainly can qualify as advertising if you are publicly discussing your professional services on your page or profile. Facebook, Google+, LinkedIn, and other social media sites can function as ads, and if so, should include all of your legally required disclosures. This can be challenging to do in a manner that visitors to your page or profile would be likely to see. You may wish to include your full title in your displayed name, so that it appears consistently at the top of the page for all visitors.

---

[333] ACA Code of Ethics, subprinciples H.5.b through H.5.d

In addition to the new web site requirements noted above, a number of the additions to the ACA Code of Ethics in 2014 centered on counselors' use of social media. Even if you are not a counselor yourself, I would encourage you to review this portion of the ACA Code as a guide to best practices in this area, as it is particularly clear and well-written. Among other requirements, the ACA Code demands that counselors keep their personal and professional social media presences separated, that they explain their social media policies (including boundaries) in the informed consent process, that they respect the privacy of clients unless given specific consent to review clients' social media profiles, and that they not disclose any confidential information through social media.[334] These are surely good standards for any mental health professional to follow.

Tweets

Twitter is a web site that allows for "micro-blogging," or posting of messages that are 140 characters or less. As you can imagine, 140 characters often do not provide enough space to include both your legally-required disclosures and whatever meaningful content you had hoped to include in a tweet.

You can advertise your practice on Twitter. You just need to use caution in doing so. The California Board of Behavioral Sciences reported in a Board meeting that they had consulted with legal counsel on therapists' use of Twitter (and Google advertising, which we will discuss next). If the BBS were to receive a complaint about such advertising, they said they would consider the totality of the advertisement. In other words, if your tweet links to your web site, they would consider the tweet and the site together.[335] As long as a potential client must have seen your legally mandated disclosures in at least one of those places, you should be safe. Another way to think of it is, do NOT include any direct contact information – like your phone number, email address, or office location – in a tweet or on your Twitter profile. If you do that, a potential client could come to you just from the tweet, never having seen your required disclosures. Instead,

---

[334] ACA Code of Ethics, subprinciples H.6.a through H.6.d
[335] California Board of Behavioral Sciences: Minutes from the July 21, 2011 meeting of the Policy and Advocacy Committee (page 6)

make sure your Twitter profile and individual tweets ONLY include a link to a web site where you *do* meet all of California's advertising disclosure requirements.

Google ads

Like tweets, Google ads provide a limited number of characters for a therapist to promote their practice. A Google ad consists of a headline (of no more than 25 characters), two lines of text (of no more than 35 characters each) and a web address for the site a user sees when they click on the ad. Again, that is not enough space for all of your legally-required disclosures, particularly if you are an intern or associate.

The same guideline applies here as applies to tweets (see above). If your Google ad contains no direct contact information, and instead leads only to a link to your web site, the BBS would consider the ad and the web site together; if your site includes all required disclosures, you should be fine. However, if your Google ad includes direct contact information like a phone number or email address, you may have prospective clients contacting you who are unsure of your licensure status, which is problematic.

▶ Professional titles

You **must** provide your licensure status in any advertising. These rules changed in 2013, so some therapists and supervisors may not be aware of the current requirements.

The law makes clear that mental health professionals must be up-front about their licensure status. **You must provide your licensure status in any advertising. As of April 1, 2013, this must be done by providing all of the following information:**

1. **Your specific license number** (for example, "LPC1234")
2. **Your full name, exactly as it is listed on your license**
3. **The fully spelled-out title of your license, or an acceptable abbreviation** (for example, "Licensed Professional Clinical Counselor" or "LPCC")[336]

The previous rules had required licensees to list their specific license number *or* their title; the new 2013 regulations require both. For more on acceptable abbreviations, see "Acronyms" later in this chapter.

References to your license should be specific to your profession. For example, you could not truthfully refer to yourself as a "licensed sex therapist," even if you were licensed as an LPCC and specializing in sex therapy, because there is not a sex therapist license in California. Similarly, there is no such thing as a "licensed intern" or "licensed associate" in California; interns and associates are *registered*, not licensed.

Additional requirements for advertising the services of prelicensed persons, particularly MFTs, are extremely specific (see "Advertisements for interns, associates, and trainees" later in this chapter).

---

[336] California Code of Regulations title 16 section 1811

Title protection

The mental health professions all enjoy what is commonly referred to as "title protection." Individuals cannot advertise themselves using the title of one of these professions unless they actually hold that license from the state of California. Even if an ad never uses the specific titles listed as protected here, it is illegal to use *any* titles, terms, or abbreviations that would lead a reasonable person to believe that an unlicensed person is actually licensed.[337]

Licensed Marriage and Family Therapists

The title "Marriage and Family Therapist" and the abbreviations "MFT" and "MFCC" are protected under state law. (MFTs were previously licensed as "marriage, family, and child counselors.") In addition, no one can advertise themselves as a "performing the services of a marriage, family, child, domestic, or marital consultant, or in any way use these or any similar titles" to imply that they perform marriage and family therapy without being licensed. Other licensed mental health professionals can say that they do marriage and family therapy, as long as such treatment is within their scope of practice.[338]

Licensed Professional Clinical Counselors

The titles "Licensed Professional Clinical Counselor," "Licensed Clinical Counselor," "Professional Clinical Counselor," and "LPCC" are all protected under the law.[339] The terms "counseling" and "counselor" by themselves are not specifically protected, and are sometimes used in other professions (including lawyers, career counselors, nutrition counselors, and so on). Other mental health professionals also sometimes refer to themselves as counselors, which is legal so long as they are not implying that they hold an LPCC license.

---

[337] California Business and Professions Code sections 4980(b), 4999.82(c), and 4996(a)
[338] California Business and Professions Code section 4980(b)
[339] California Business and Professions Code section 4999.82(b)

Licensed Clinical Social Workers

The title "Licensed Clinical Social Worker" is specifically protected under state law. As with the other professions, it is also illegal to use any other term or title that suggests you are an LCSW unless you hold that license.[340] Other mental health professions can do work of a psychosocial nature, but cannot present themselves with titles that include "psychosocial" or "Clinical Social Worker."[341]

Acronyms

State regulations currently require the use of both the license number and a license title or acceptable abbreviation in advertising. Below are the acronyms that are acceptable to distinguish different licensure types:[342]

MFT or LMFT: Licensed Marriage and Family Therapist.
MFTI: Marriage and Family Therapist Registered Intern.*
LPCC: Licensed Professional Clinical Counselor.
PCCI: Professional Clinical Counselor Intern.*
LCSW: Licensed Clinical Social Worker.

* Prelicensed therapists have additional requirements when they use acronyms in place of their full registration titles. For more on this, see "Advertisements for interns, associates, and trainees" later in this chapter.

Note that there is *no* acceptable acronym for social work associates.[343] It is also worth noting here that **neither law nor common practice allows for any abbreviation of the term "trainee" in any of the mental health professions.** I have occasionally seen (with great concern) MFT trainees using the abbreviation "MFTT" to denote their title. This would almost certainly be seen as an attempt to mislead regarding one's trainee status. If you are a trainee, always spell out the word when giving your title.

---

[340] California Business and Professions Code section 4996(a)
[341] California Business and Professions Code section 4996.13
[342] California Code of Regulations title 16 section 1811
[343] California Code of Regulations title 16 section 1811

Fictitious business names

As with other businesses, therapists can use fictitious business names to refer to their practices. It is common for group practices to take on a singular name for the practice (for example, "Neighborhood Therapy Group") rather than listing each individual therapist in the name of the business. However, such fictitious names cannot be false or misleading ("Neighborhood Clinical Psychology Services" would be false if the therapists there were not Psychologists), and any client coming to a therapy practice that operates under a fictitious business name has to be informed of the owners' names and licensure status prior to the beginning of treatment.[344]

"Psychotherapy" and "psychotherapist"

As of April 1, 2013, professionals licensed by the BBS can use the terms "psychotherapy" and "psychotherapist" in their advertisements provided that they have included all of the required information listed above (license number, full name as it is listed on your license, and your license title or an acceptable abbreviation).[345]

The regulations on this issue specifically apply to licensees, leaving the matter unclear for interns and associates. However, MFT interns, PCC interns, and CSW associates are all defined as psychotherapists in other places in the law.[346] So, some interns and associates simply follow the same guidelines, also including all of the other legally required disclosures for their ads (see "Advertisements for interns, associates, and trainees" later in this chapter). However, you may wish to consult with your supervisor and an attorney before doing so.

---

[344] California Business and Professions Code section 4980.46
[345] California Code of Regulations title 16 section 1811
[346] As two examples, California Business and Professions Code section 728(c)(1) and California Evidence Code section 1010 both include interns and associates in their definitions of the term "psychotherapist." However, these definitions are clear in specifying that they only apply to their sections of law, so it may be inappropriate to interpret them as having any meaning relevant to advertising rules.

You should avoid terms "licensed psychotherapist," "licensed behavioral therapist," "licensed couple therapist," and so on. These terms could be considered false because there are no such licenses in California.

▶ Professional qualifications

> **Therapists are encouraged, but not required, to put additional information about their qualifications in advertising.** When such information is included, it must be accurate and relevant.

In addition to the required information about licensure status, therapists often include additional information in their ads to show prospective clients that they are well qualified to provide particular types of treatment. **None of this information is required to be in an advertisement,** but the law and some professional ethical codes encourage informing clients as fully as possible about your education, training, and experience. Prospective clients often find it helpful in making informed choices about whom to call. When information about professional qualifications is included in ads, the law does include requirements that the information be truthful and relevant.

Degrees

Legally, **you can advertise any earned degree from an accredited or approved university so long as it is relevant to the discipline in which you are working.** If you have a master's degree in counseling and a PhD in physics, you could not advertise your counseling services using "PhD" after your name.

The law does not specify where it is or is not acceptable to include the word "doctor" or the abbreviation "Dr." It should go without saying that any such usage that creates a mistaken belief that you are trained or licensed as a medical doctor would be illegal. If you have a doctorate degree relevant to your practice, however, the rules are less clear. While I am not an attorney, it would seem far safer to advertise the specific degree type (by putting "Ph.D." after your name, for example) than to use "doctor" in any context where it might be misunderstood.

Some therapists in doctoral degree programs use the initials "ABD" to indicate that they have completed coursework requirements for the doctorate degree. ("ABD" stands for "All But Dissertation.") Since this is not a formal license or degree status, it is better not to include this in any advertising.

Specializations

State law does not specifically mention the advertising of specializations. However, professional codes of ethics prohibit a therapist from working in or advertising an area of specialization unless the therapist has appropriate training, education, experience, or combination thereof, to ensure competency in the specialization.[347] It could be considered misleading to advertise a specialization in an area where you have an interest but no additional training or experience to speak of.

When advertising a specialization, you also should bear in mind that such an advertisement may obligate you to a higher standard of care while working in that area; clients could reasonably expect that your skills and services within that specialization would be comparable to other therapists *who share that specialization*, and not simply other therapists in general.[348]

Certifications

Many private organizations offer certifications in specific areas of training. These certifications are not regulated by the state, and no outside certification is necessary to practice in any area that is within your legal scope of practice. However, as with other qualifications you hold, you cannot advertise yourself as certified in a particular area of practice unless you actually hold that certification.

It is also important to bear in mind that being "certified" to perform a particular type of treatment is not the same as having a continuing education (CE) *certificate* from a particular training. In other words, going to a two-hour training on motivational interviewing, and receiving a certificate for the CE hours, does not mean you can list yourself as "certified" in the motivational interviewing approach. (You can, of course, truthfully say you have attended the training.)

---

[347] AAMFT Code of Ethics subprinciple 9.7; ACA Code of Ethics subprinciple C.2.b; NASW Code of Ethics subprinciple 1.04(b)
[348] Pelchat, Z. (2001 May/June). The standard of care: Definitions and examples. *The Therapist.*

Association membership

If it is true, it is legal to include in an advertisement that you are a member of your professional association. Be warned, however, that some associations specifically require in their Codes of Ethics that any advertising mentioning your membership also clearly indicate what type of member you are (student member, associate member, or clinical member, for example).[349] In addition, presenting the initials of your association after your name as if it were an academic degree or a license (for example, "John Doe, LPCC, *ACA*") could be considered misleading.

---

[349] ACA Code of Ethics subrinciple C.4.f; CAMFT Code of Ethics subprinciple 10.9

▶ Advertising content

> **The same laws that apply to other businesses' advertisements also apply to therapists.** False or misleading claims about you or your competitors are not allowed. Other restrictions also apply.

The state laws that apply to all business advertising also apply to therapists. You cannot produce ads that are fraudulent, that make false claims about you or your competitors, and so on. There are some additional laws that apply more specifically to ads by or for health care professionals, including psychotherapists.

Claims of effectiveness

As a general rule, you should avoid making any claims in advertising psychotherapy that could be construed as a guarantee (for example, "feeling depressed? Therapy will help!"). Even the best therapies do not *always* work. Even if you are not intending to lie or mislead, the law prohibits any claim that "is likely to create false or unjustified expectations of favorable results."[350] This is why it is common for therapists' ads to use language noting that their therapy "can be" or "could be" an effective way to resolve a particular problem, not that it "will be."

If you make specific claims of effectiveness for a method or technique you use (for example, if you say that your method has been shown to work in 4 out of 5 cases), you must be able to back up those claims with published, peer-reviewed studies of the method or technique.[351]

---

[350] California Business and Professions Code section 651(b)(3)(A)
[351] California Business and Professions Code section 651(b)(7)

Fees

Clients must be informed of the fee and how it was computed prior to the beginning of services.[352] While ads do not need to include fee information, many therapists choose to include this information in their advertising. This must be done with caution, however, especially if you operate on a sliding fee scale. **The law requires that advertisements including prices be exact.** The law does not allow ads to include terms like "as low as," "and up," "lowest prices," or anything similar.[353] Therapists or agencies working on sliding fee scales should be cautious to avoid misleading all clients into believing they will get the lowest fee.

Testimonials

California law prohibits advertisements from including any testimonials that are likely to create false expectations in the eyes of consumers.[354] Professional codes of ethics go farther than this, specifically declaring it unethical for mental health professionals to solicit testimonials of any kind from their clients.[355] While a professional code of ethics does not carry the same weight as state law, it is a reference point that the BBS uses when seeking to determine whether a therapist has engaged in unprofessional conduct.

Questions surrounding testimonials have grown more complex in the age of Yelp, Angie's List, Health Grades, and similar web sites where clients may openly post about their experiences with particular therapists. While other types of businesspeople will sometimes respond to negative reviews on these sites, therapists rarely do so, out of concern for the client's confidentiality. Of course, in posting a review, a client may be telling the world that they have been in therapy with you – but that does not give the therapist permission to go online and discuss anything about the client's therapy.

---

[352] California Code of Regulations title 16 section 1881(j)
[353] California Business and Professions Code section 651(c)
[354] California Business and Professions Code section 651(b)(8)
[355] ACA Code of Ethics subprinciple C.3.b; CAMFT Code of Ethics subprinciple 10.6; NASW Code of Ethics subprinciple 4.07(b)

▶ Advertisements for interns, associates, and trainees

> **Ads for therapists who are not yet licensed must include specific additional disclosures.**

As previously mentioned, interns and associates are allowed to advertise their services if they include additional specific disclosures.[356] Trainees cannot advertise themselves, but their employers can place advertisements on the trainees' behalf.

Before we address the additional disclosure requirements for ads that discuss the services of trainees and registrants, a common question:

Who pays for ads for interns and associates?

For interns and associates, the question often arises of who is expected to pay for advertising of their services. While the law disallows MFT interns and CSW associates from renting their own office space, buying their own furniture, buying equipment, or paying for any other "obligations of their employers," the law does not name advertising as an employer's expense.[357] As such, it seems that interns and associates can pay for their own advertising. However, because the law is not specific, it is helpful to have a clear advance agreement with your supervisor that specifies who will be paying for what when it comes to marketing costs.

---

[356] California Code of Regulations title 16 section 1811
[357] California Business and Professions Code sections 4980.43(i) and 4996.23(l)(3). There is no similar language for PCC interns, who are simply restricted from having a proprietary interest in the employer's business (section 4999.47(f)).

Clinical Social Worker associates and trainees

Registered associate Clinical Social Workers are specifically allowed to advertise under the law. They must use either the fully spelled-out title "Registered Associate Clinical Social Worker" or the abbreviation "Registered Associate CSW." The law does not allow for the use of "ACSW" or other acronyms.[358] Social work associates' ads must not be false, fraudulent, misleading, or otherwise deceptive,[359] and they must specify that the associate is unlicensed and under supervision.[360]

There are not advertising laws specific to trainees, who cannot advertise their own services. Agencies and organizations advertising trainees' services typically do so cautiously, making it clear what services trainees provide.

Marriage and Family Therapist Registered Interns

Any advertising by or on behalf of an MFT intern must include all of the following:

1. The complete title "Marriage and Family Therapist Registered Intern" or the abbreviation "MFT Registered Intern"
2. The intern's registration number
3. The name of the intern's employer
4. That the intern is supervised by a licensed person[361]

In a private practice setting, the employer and the supervisor would be the same person, so providing their name and license number would meet the requirements of both #3 and #4 above. It would make sense to say something like "Employed and Supervised by" followed by the supervisor's name and license number. In an agency setting, the same intern may have multiple supervisors or there may be frequent supervisor turnover, so it is sufficient to provide the

---

[358] California Code of Regulations title 16 section 1811
[359] California Business and Professions Code section 4992.3(q)
[360] California Business and Professions Code section 4996.18(h)
[361] California Business and Professions Code section 4980.44(d)

name of the employing agency (#3) and a statement that the intern is under licensed supervision (#4).

Under current law, the "MFTI" abbreviation can never be used on its own. It can only appear in an advertisement that also includes the fully spelled-out title "Marriage and Family Therapist Registered Intern." The abbreviated title "MFT Registered Intern" does *not* meet the requirement here – if you want to call yourself an MFTI in an ad, you must also call yourself a "Marriage and Family Therapist Registered Intern."[362]

Marriage and Family Therapist trainees

California law for MFTs includes two somewhat different standards for advertising the services provided by trainees. Until the law is clarified, it would seem safest to ensure that advertising of trainees' services meets *both* sets of standards. Under this rationale, any advertising by or on behalf of an MFT trainee must include all of the following:

1. The trainee's name
2. That the person is a Marriage and Family Therapist trainee
3. The name of the trainee's employer
4. That the trainee is supervised by a licensed person
5. The supervisor's license type or abbreviation, and license number[363]

Providing the name and license number of the supervisor would seem to meet the requirements of #4 as well as #5. The most important change from prior law is the inclusion of the employer's name, which was not required before 2012.

---

[362] California Code of Regulations title 16 section 1811
[363] California Business and Professions Code section 4980.48(b) and (c)

Professional Clinical Counselor Registered Interns

Clinical counselor interns' ads must not be false, fraudulent, misleading, or otherwise deceptive.[364] Their ads must include the therapist's name, their registration number, and the full title "Professional Clinical Counselor Registered Intern" or the abbreviation "PCC Registered Intern." The acronym "PCCI" can only be used in an ad that *also* uses the full and exact title "Professional Clinical Counselor Registered Intern."[365]

Advertisements for counselor interns must also include the name of the employer (or, if it is a volunteer setting, the name of the organization). While the law does not technically require counselor interns to indicate that they are under supervision in their advertising, it certainly makes sense to do so. Clients must be informed that the intern is unlicensed and under supervision before any services are provided.[366] In a private practice setting, it would make sense to say something like "Employed and Supervised by" followed by the supervisor's name and license number.

Professional Clinical Counselor trainees

Clinical counselor trainees are required to inform clients prior to the beginning of treatment that they are unlicensed and under supervision.[367] Ads on behalf of clinical counselor trainees regularly include this information. As with the other professions, clinical counselor trainees cannot advertise on their own.

---

[364] California Business and Professions Code section 4999.90(p)
[365] California Code of Regulations title 16 section 1811
[366] California Business and Professions Code section 4999.45(c)
[367] California Business and Professions Code section 4999.36(d)

▶ Networking groups

Some clinicians choose to participate in networking groups to help spread the word about their services. These groups typically aim to bring together businesspeople representing a wide variety of goods and services in a specific local area, for the purpose of exchanging referral information on potential customers.

The aims of these groups are very positive. If you know someone who needs a plumber, a dentist, a computer expert, or any other service, wouldn't you rather send them to someone you know than simply have them pick a name out of the phone book or a Google search? Networking groups often serve to build trust and community among those who work in the same area, and can do so very effectively.

These groups can also represent dangerous territory for therapists, however. Such groups may require that when you make or receive a referral within the group, information on the prospective customer be recorded by a group administrator who tracks referrals, raising confidentiality concerns. More worrisome are those groups that reward referrals or penalize group members who don't make a certain number of referrals to other group members each year. Recall from chapter 3 that state law specifically prohibits paying, accepting, or soliciting a fee for referrals.[368] Even if the reward for referrals within the group is simply avoidance of what would otherwise be a financial penalty, it could still be argued that you are, in essence, receiving a fee for referrals by not having to pay.

It may be helpful here to consider why the rules against fees for referrals exist. The idea is to make sure that clients can be fully confident our referrals are based solely on *what is best for them*, and not in any way on what is best for *us*. When we receive a direct personal benefit from referring a client out to another professional, it raises at least the *appearance* of a conflict of interests. That undermines the credibility not just of the individual therapist or that specific referral, but of *every* referral made by that therapist – and arguably, any referral made by any therapist.

---

[368] California Business and Professions Code sections 4982(o), 4992.3(p), and 4999.90(o)

Networking groups can be very useful if they allow you to get to know other local businesspeople, to make presentations about your services, and to exchange business cards and other marketing information about your practice. But if membership in such a group requires making a certain number of referrals each year, if you would receive payment (or avoid financial penalties) for making referrals to others within the group, or if referral information has to go through a group administrator, participating in such a group may not be worth the risk.

9

Technology

Cell phones, the Internet, and videoconferencing technology have made it easier than ever for clients to access mental health services. At the same time, using these technologies presents added risk when it comes to protecting your client's confidentiality. California has specific laws surrounding the use of technology for psychotherapy and supervision. Federal law impacts such services as well. Professional ethical codes are also beginning to more directly address technology.

▸ Understanding telehealth

If you utilize the telephone, Internet, or videoconferencing in the delivery of mental health services, you are engaging in what is now called "telehealth." (The term was changed to "telehealth" in state law in 2011,[369] but many practitioners are more familiar with the older term "telemedicine.") More technically, telehealth involves the delivery of health care services through interactive audio, video, or data connections.[370] The term "delivery of services" is important – simply using the phone or email for routine administrative contacts, such as appointment scheduling, is not considered to be within the definition of telehealth.[371]

Telehealth offers a number of potential advantages to both consumers and therapists, particularly regarding access to care. Clients in rural areas or with specific language needs can access qualified providers via telehealth without having to drive for hours for each therapy session. Providers can expand their practices beyond their local communities, which is especially helpful if you serve a highly specific clientele or specialize in working with less-common problems.

However, telehealth also brings with it a number of potential problems. The therapist needs to be skilled in utilizing the technology, of course, and also must be prepared to address emergency situations for clients who may not be located in areas the therapist is familiar with. There are also concerns about privacy and confidentiality of client data.

In spite of these concerns, telehealth is increasingly practiced among mental health providers. In a 2011 survey, more than half of CAMFT members said they provided at least some of their services via telehealth.[372] As we saw in Chapter 2 (Licensing Requirements), all three of the professions covered in this text are able to gather a portion of their hours of experience for licensure by providing services by phone or Internet.

---

[369] Assembly Bill 415 (2011)

[370] California Business and Professions Code section 2290.5

[371] Atkins, C. (2011 November/December). A 2011 recap of the 1996 Telemedicine Development Act. *The Therapist.*

[372] Atkins, C. (2011 November/December). A 2011 recap of the 1996 Telemedicine Development Act. *The Therapist.*

While our focus in this text is California law, it is helpful to understand the federal laws and ethical rules governing telehealth to ensure that you are providing telehealth services in an appropriate manner if you are going to offer these services at all. In this chapter, we focus on California's rules, but also briefly review the requirements found in professional ethical codes and some of the rules found in federal law. As is the case with the rest of this book, the coverage here is not meant to be all-inclusive. You also should keep in mind that both technology and the rules surrounding its use can change quickly.

If you are interested in providing services via telehealth, you may want to become familiar with some of the businesses and professional organizations that specifically work in this area.[373] The American Telemedicine Association regularly publishes best-practice guidelines for telehealth practitioners in a variety of areas; their 2013 guidelines of vide-based mental health care offer useful and highly specific guidance on security protocols, bandwidth, and much more.[374] The Online Therapy Institute trains exclusively in this area, and offers a number of certifications for online practitioners.[375] MyTherapyNet is an example of a platform that aims to provide secure and legally-compliant videoconferencing connections between therapists and the clients they serve.[376] And SimplePractice is one of several companies specializing in handling therapists' scheduling, billing, and documentation in a secure manner.[377]

Ultimately, if you are interested in providing services via telehealth, there is no shortage of individuals and groups eager to train you for such practice, provide the platform for connecting, and assist you with the administrative elements. Just remember that the ultimate responsibility is on you to ensure that your practice stays current with all legal and ethical requirements.

---

[373] As is the case with all references to outside groups in this book, please do not take this paragraph as an endorsement of these organizations or as an indication that they endorse this book. These are just intended to give you a sense of the kinds of resources available if you want to learn more about telehealth. Of course, this is by no means an exhaustive list.

[374] www.americantelemed.org

[375] onlinetherapyinstitute.com

[376] mytherapynet.com

[377] www.simplepractice.com

▶ Legal requirements when providing services by telehealth

Both state and federal law establish requirements surrounding therapists' use of technology. The California Telemedicine Act and the later California Telemedicine Advancement Act have the most direct rules for working with patients, while other state laws address the use of technology in supervision. Federal laws (including the Health Insurance Portability and Accountability Act, or HIPAA, and the Health Information Technology for Economic and Clinical Health Act, or HITECH) also govern telehealth services provided by mental health clinicians. This text focuses on state law, so the discussion of HIPAA and HITECH here is only a very brief overview.

The California Telemedicine Act

As mentioned above, there are two primary pieces of state legislation that govern telemedicine in California: The California Telemedicine Act of 1996 and the California Telemedicine Advancement Act of 2011.[378] These bills recognized the growing role of technology in the delivery of health care services, and sought to ensure insurers and health care organizations, including Medi-Cal, would pay for such services. However, these are not the only state laws to advance telehealth. The California Telehealth Resource Center[379] offers a complete history of state legislation and ballot initiatives that have shaped our current telehealth laws.[380]

The California Telemedicine Act and most related laws are not specific to psychotherapy, covering instead a wide scope of health care services. A 2003 law clarified that the state's telemedicine rules do apply to mental health practitioners.[381] While these laws focus largely on billing and payment, and are not the only telehealth rules in

---

[378] Senate Bill 1665 (1996) and Assembly Bill 415 (2011)

[379] California Telehealth Resource Center. While their site is government-funded through a grant, note that this is part of a nonprofit organization, and not an official government site.

[380] California Telehealth Resource Center: California legislation

[381] Assembly Bill 116 (2003)

California law, the consent process is particularly important for therapists to know and follow when working in telehealth:

- Prior to any service delivery by telehealth, the client must be informed that telehealth services will be used
- The client must give verbal consent for telehealth services
- The client's verbal consent must be written in the client's record[382]

Note that these requirements are above and beyond the standard requirements for informed consent for therapy, which were discussed in Chapter 4 (Informed Consent).

Using technology in supervision

Just as technology can make it easier for a client to find a therapist especially well-suited to the client's needs, it also can make it easier for a clinic to find a well-qualified supervisor for their prelicensed therapists. Noting the difficulty many interns and associates have in finding supervision, especially in rural areas, the BBS has supported changes in law that made it legal for most work settings (*except* private practices, where supervision *must* be provided in person) to use videoconferencing for supervision.[383] This rule applies only to registrants, however; trainees must be supervised in person.

HIPAA

HIPAA places a number of requirements on therapists who are governed by it. It is important to note, however, that not all therapists are required to follow the HIPAA rules. You are considered to be a "covered entity" if you transmit sensitive health information electronically for the purposes of billing, referrals, eligibility inquiries,

---

[382] California Business and Professions Code section 2290.5(b)
[383] California Business and Professions Code sections 4980.43(c)(6), 4996.23(c)(6) and 4999.46(g)(4)

or a number of other covered transactions.[384] If you are a part of a clinic or organization that is covered by HIPAA, you are obligated to follow the law, even if you personally do not transmit information electronically.

The rules put in place by HIPAA are quite complex, reflecting the law's effort to balance protecting the privacy of individuals with allowing the free flow of information needed for effective care and for analysis of providers. Thankfully, there are a number of excellent reference guides on the rules of HIPAA available to you. I particularly recommend the Heath Information Privacy section on the Department of Health and Human Services' web site.[385]

HHS breaks down HIPAA into three key rules for practitioners, and I've added a fourth to emphasize an important new component (numbers and emphasis added):

1. "The **HIPAA Privacy Rule**, which protects the privacy of individually identifiable health information;
2. The **HIPAA Security Rule**, which sets national standards for the security of electronic protected health information; and
3. The **confidentiality provisions of the Patient Safety Rule**, which protect identifiable information being used to analyze patient safety events and improve patient safety."[386]
4. The **Breach Notification Rule**, which requires providers to inform HHS of data security breaches and to inform those patients whose data has been breached.

The HIPAA Privacy Rule

The HIPAA Privacy Rule protects all identifiable information about a client, including common identifiers (like name and birthdate), information about their health care treatment, and information about their payment for services. Health information that has been de-identified – that is, all personally identifiable information

---

[384] Office of Civil Rights, U.S. Department of Health and Human Services: Summary of the HIPAA Privacy Rule
[385] http://www.hhs.gov/ocr/privacy/
[386] Office of Civil Rights, U.S. Department of Health and Human Services: Health Information Privacy

has been removed – is not protected under the HIPAA Privacy Rule.[387] This allows for health care providers to give data sets to researchers for research purposes. Several recent studies comparing mental health professions' effectiveness in treating various problems have relied on large, de-identified data sets from health care organizations.

If you are part of a covered entity, you must protect your clients' information in accordance with HIPAA. Among your requirements are:

- Developing and implementing privacy policies and procedures
- Designate a privacy official responsible for maintaining adherence to the policy and handling complaints
- Training all staff members on your privacy policy and procedures
- Formally disciplining staff members who violate the privacy policy
- Repairing any harmful effects of violations of the privacy policy
- Maintaining specific reasonable safeguards to protect against the release of private information
- Having procedures for clients to make formal complaints about violations of privacy
- Maintaining records of the privacy policy, all complaints, and related information for at least six years

These requirements apply even if you are an individual working in a private practice. You would still need to develop formal written policies for the protection of private information, and for clients to make complaints, along with all of the requirements listed earlier in this chapter and others spelled out in the law. While this may at first appear to be a significant burden, a therapist in private practice who is thoughtful in maintaining privacy is unlikely to need to handle complaints very often.

---

[387] Office of Civil Rights, U.S. Department of Health and Human Services: Summary of the HIPAA Privacy Rule

The HIPAA Security Rule

The Privacy Rule described above applies to client information in all forms, including in writing. In contrast, the HIPAA Security Rule applies specifically to client information that is created, received, transmitted, or maintained in *electronic* formats.[388]

The therapist or organization covered by HIPAA must respond to the Security Rule by:

- Ensuring the confidentiality, integrity, and availability (to appropriate persons) of all electronic health information
- Protecting against anticipated threats to the security of any electronic health information
- Protecting against anticipated improper uses or disclosures of electronic health information
- Ensuring compliance with this rule by all staff[389]

In another contrast with the Privacy Rule, the Security Rule acknowledges that there are meaningful differences between the protections that will need to be put in place by a large organization (like a hospital) and those that will need to be put in place by a single individual (like a therapist in private practice). In either case, given the rapid changes in technology, the provider must regularly review and update their practices to best protect the security of electronic health information.[390]

Confidentiality provisions of the Patient Safety Rule

While the rules generally move toward the protection of private health information, the government also recognizes the importance of understanding the safety records of various health care facilities. For example, there is great value in knowing whether your

---

[388] Office of Civil Rights, U.S. Department of Health and Human Services: Summary of the HIPAA Security Rule
[389] Office of Civil Rights, U.S. Department of Health and Human Services: Summary of the HIPAA Security Rule
[390] Office of Civil Rights, U.S. Department of Health and Human Services: Summary of the HIPAA Security Rule

risk of death from infection is higher at one hospital than another. In order to make that kind of a determination, patient records must be made available for research and analysis.

The Patient Safety Rule, added to HIPAA in 2009, establishes a voluntary system for the reporting and analysis of safety events. Most mental health providers will not be impacted by this rule. However, if you work for a large organization such as a hospital or large clinic, your organization may participate in the voluntary reporting system. Under the confidentiality provisions of the Patient Safety Rule, information used in the reporting and analysis of safety events is considered both confidential and privileged under federal law.[391]

The Breach Notification Rule

Under new rules taking effect in September 2013, all HIPAA-covered entities must monitor their systems for breaches of unsecured health information, and report such breaches to HHS as well as to the clients whose information was potentially impacted. Breaches do not have to be intentional; if your computer or cell phone contains unencrypted client information and is stolen, that may be a reportable breach, even if you have no way of knowing whether the protected data was actually accessed. Data breaches involving fewer than 500 clients are reported on an annual basis. Larger breaches have more immediate and complicated reporting requirements.[392]

HITECH

While HIPAA works largely to protect patients by *restricting* how health information can be shared electronically, HITECH is a law largely designed to *facilitate* the sharing of electronic health records. At least in theory, if more health care practitioners are using electronic medical records with consistent standards, it should be easier for

---

[391] Office of Civil Rights, U.S. Department of Health and Human Services: Understanding Patient Safety Confidentiality
[392] American Psychological Association (2014). *Are you aware of HIPAA breach notification standards?* Available online at www.apapracticecentral.org/update/2014/10-23/hipaa-breach.aspx

practitioners to obtain necessary medical information about a patient's history. This is especially important in an emergency.

One way the HITECH act encourages the use of electronic health records is with financial rewards and punishments for physicians and other providers who accept federal funding through Medicare and Medicaid. For eligible providers, there were rewards for adopting electronic health records early, and punishments for those who are not meaningfully using electronic health records as of 2015 (with increasing penalties in future years). These provisions do *not* apply to mental health professionals, though the American Psychological Association has argued that they should.[393]

One part of HITECH strengthens the enforcement provisions of HIPAA, increasing the criminal and civil penalties that can be used when a health care provider or organization fails to appropriately protect electronic health records. HITECH also strengthened the government's ability to enforce HIPAA requirements on the companies we rely on for the creation and storage of electronic health records.

As of September 2013, therapists who are covered by HIPAA must ensure that any third party they use to store or transmit protected health information *also* follows the HIPAA requirements to which the therapist is bound. The safest companies for a HIPAA-covered therapist to work with are those who are willing to sign a HIPAA Business Associate Agreement, a document attesting that they meet (and, importantly, plan to continue to meet) legal requirements for data privacy and security. The Department of Health and Human Services has a great deal of information online about when these agreements are necessary and what responsibilities a therapist has relative to their business associates.[394]

---

[393] American Psychological Association (2012). *The HITECH Act and eligible professionals: FAQ for psychologists.* Available online at www.apapracticecentral.org/update/2012/07-30/hitech-act.aspx
[394] www.hhs.gov/ocr/privacy/hipaa/faq/smaller_providers_and_businesses offers a lengthy and helpful list of common questions and their answers, though note that it is relevant to smaller providers like a private practice or a small clinic. Larger clinics, hospitals, and other larger practices are held to more stringent guidelines, since they are responsible for protecting more health information.

▶ Ethical requirements when providing services by telehealth

While this book focuses on state law in California, it is worth noting here that the legal guidelines above are not the only standards to follow when providing services via electronic technology. The professional ethics codes of all three major mental health professions covered in this text have moved toward specific additional requirements for therapists providing services through such technology. The American Counseling Association's code is the most specific, though many of its requirements are effectively duplicated in the codes of the other associations.

The chart below outlines how each of the associations has tackled issues surrounding therapist use of technology. Bear in mind that the fact that something is not discussed specifically does not mean the therapist is free from that obligation. For example, the ACA Code of Ethics does not directly provide specific added guidelines for the electronic storage of client records, beyond that the therapist should follow the law and also should inform clients about the security and length of electronic record storage.[395] However, other parts of the ACA Code would suggest that a therapist would take precautions with electronic records that they may not take with paper records. Subprinciple B.6.b requires counselors to "ensure that records and documentation kept in any medium are kept in a secure location and that only authorized persons have access to them."[396] Ensuring security and limited access would logically seem to logically require more precautions for electronic records than paper records.

Note that the references to specific subprinciples in Table 9.1 are only the most *directly* applicable to that issue; other subprinciples within that association's Code of Ethics may apply, regardless of whether the task is listed by name in the code. All of the listed tasks are certainly good practices for all mental health professionals using technology.

---

[395] ACA Code of Ethics subprinciple H.5.a
[396] ACA Code of Ethics subprinciple B.6.b

Table 9.1: Ethical requirements for use of technology*

Therapist is required to...	Included in Association's Code of Ethics?[397]			
	AAMFT	CAMFT	ACA	NASW
...inform client of benefits and limitations of using technology	Yes 6.1(b)	Yes 1.4.2	Yes H.4.a	Yes 1.03e
...determine that technology-based services are appropriate to client needs and abilities	Yes 6.1(a)		Yes H.4.c	
...consider face-to-face services if technology-based services are ineffective			Yes H.4.d	
...provide reasonable access to computer applications			Yes H.4.e	
...ensure that all use of technology is in keeping with applicable law	Yes 6.1	Yes 3.11	Yes H.1.b	
...ensure that electronic communications with the client are appropriately secured	Yes 6.1(c)		Yes H.2.d	
...be appropriately trained in the use of the specific technology used to provide service	Yes 6.1(d), 6.6		Yes H.1.a	
...provide specific additional informed consent and disclosure (information needed varies by association)	Yes 6.2, 6.3	Yes 1.4.2	Yes H.2.a	
...provide an emergency process to follow if the therapist is not available		Yes 1.5.3	Yes H.2.a	
...adhere to additional standards for web sites and social media			Yes H.5, H.6	
...reasonably protect confidentiality of information transmitted electronically	Yes 2.7	Yes 2.3	Yes H.2.b	Yes 1.07m
...reasonably protect the security of records stored electronically	Yes 6.4		Yes H.5.a	Yes 1.07l

Notes: (1) Specific wording of the required tasks varies by association. (2) The absence of a "yes" in any particular box should NOT be interpreted to mean that the therapist does not need to do the listed task. Rather, it only means that the task is not specifically mandated in that ethics code. The task may be reasonably required by subprinciples in the code that do not mention the task by name.

---

[397] See Appendix for links to each organization's full Codes of Ethics.

▶ Communicating with clients

As discussed above, a phone call with a client for administrative purposes like scheduling the next session would not qualify as telehealth since you are not actually providing therapy services on that call. However, electronic data transmission and storage -- including storage of protected health information -- is now so common that it often happens without our taking conscious action to make it happen. This is important to consider when you weigh the best ways to keep in touch with your clients.

Email

Under new HIPAA requirements taking effect in late 2013, therapists covered by HIPAA must inform their clients and get specific consent for communicating with clients via unsecured email. (As a general rule, your email is unsecured; a few secured-email providers have sprung up in recent years, but very few people use them, and you generally have to pay to use such a service.) This rule caused therapists some alarm, though it generally just means you need to acknowledge to your clients that there's risk inherent in sending messages this way.[398]

In my experience, clients tend to welcome a brief discussion of email security. They appreciate that I am thinking of their privacy, and it can be a helpful reminder to them to use privacy options like two-factor authentication. Whether you are a HIPAA-covered entity or not, it is worth giving careful consideration to what kinds of information you will discuss over email, and making sure clients are aware of your email-related policies.

Consider what happens to email once it is sent. Many of us, myself included, now use email providers that basically never require deleting old messages -- meaning that, if you discuss clinical information via email, there is the potential for protected health

---

[398] This article offers a common-sense approach: www.personcenteredtech.com/2013/10/clients-have-the-right-to-receive-unencrypted-emails-under-hipaa/

information to remain in your account forever, always susceptible to prying eyes of outsiders if your email account is hacked.

Texting

Texting can provide added convenience for therapists and clients alike. It can bring clients peace of mind to know that they can text you to let you know that they are running 10 minutes late for their session. Again, though, it is worth giving careful thought to what kind of information will ultimately be stored on your phone (and on the cloud, if you regularly back up your phone using a cloud-based service). Text messages are typically unsecured, which arguably goes against new ethical standards from AAMFT and ACA requiring reasonable security protections for all forms of electronic communication (see Table 9.1).

Perhaps more concerning, if a phone you have used to text with clients is lost or stolen, whoever is lucky enough to find it may be able to access a great deal of information about those you work with. Simple password protection does not qualify as encryption of this kind of data, meaning that even a password-protected phone may need to be reported as a data breach if it contains client information.

The intention here is not to scare you into thinking we should all go back to the time of telegrams or carrier pigeons. *No* form of communication is entirely secure. It is precisely because electronic communication is so easy to *not* think about that we have an added duty to think about it, to act as careful stewards of health information on our clients' behalf.

As is the case with email, if you plan to communicate with clients via text, it can be helpful to make sure clients are very clear on your policies for such communication and how you protect their information. Some have speculated that texting will be the focus of the next wave of HIPAA enforcement standards. Perhaps better, HHS could aid in the development of a secure standard for text messaging of health information.[399]

---

[399] Department of Health and Human Services (HHS) Text4Health Task Force (n.d.). *Health text messaging recommendations to the secretary.* Available online at www.hhs.gov/open/initiatives/mhealth/recommendations.html

▸ Technology issues in other parts of this book

Advanced electronic technology is woven into our lives. There is a good chance that you do not leave the house without your cell phone. When you look for a plumber or contractor for your home, you are likely searching on the Internet (or, increasingly, you may be doing that on your phone as well). We utilize technology in our lives and in our practices often without even thinking about it.

This book is no exception. Technology is now so woven into the work of professional therapists that issues surrounding electronic communications have been discussed in almost every chapter. Consider, as just one example, that mandated reports of elder and dependent adult abuse can now be filed via Internet in some counties, as discussed in Chapter 7.

So, at least a couple of reminders are in order here. These were discussed in other parts of this book, but are particularly relevant in discussions of technology in mental health services:

1. Licensure stops at the state line

A reminder is in order here: as we discussed back in Chapter 1, your license only allows you to see clients who are physically located within the state of California at the time of service. If your client is in another state, and you are working with them via phone or Internet, the other state could see you as practicing there without a license.

2. Online advertising is still advertising

As we saw in Chapter 8, therapists are marketing their services online in a variety of settings. Facebook, Twitter, and the like can seem to blur the lines of what exactly qualifies as an "advertisement;" in the eyes of the law, however, the term is defined very broadly, to include any public discussion of your services.

10

Advocating for Changes in Law, Regulation, or Policy

It is easy to forget that the laws, regulations, and policies that govern our work are written and enforced by people just like you and me. These rules are constantly evolving in response to the changing needs of the professions and the populations we serve, and any individual practitioner or student can have an impact on them. In this chapter, I focus on how to identify problems with existing laws, regulations, and policies, and how to work to change them. You may be surprised at just how easy it can be for one person to make a real difference.

▶ Our calling to influence policy

Licensed mental health professionals are recognized and respected as being the community's experts on human functioning. While doctors are looked to for physical health and lawyers are looked to for knowledge of the rules of society, mental health professionals are rightly seen as uniquely educated and experienced in resolving interpersonal problems and reducing human suffering.

So why don't we have more impact on the law?

In short, not enough of us are working to have that impact. Policymakers are eager to hear from us and want to do what is best for the health of their constituents.

I realize that may arouse skepticism in some readers. When I started doing advocacy work, I certainly had that skepticism. But having now done advocacy work in some form or another for about 10 years, I can say with pleasant surprise that this has absolutely been my experience. In most cases, I only know state legislators' party affiliations from what I have read about them elsewhere; I have experienced every policymaker and staffer I have met as trying to do what is right for the people of their districts, regardless of party affiliation. They have a real and genuine hunger for facts and expertise, and often wish they had more of it from mental health professionals. Multiple surveys of legislators from various parts of the country back this up: Policymakers want to hear from us.

The failing is on our end.

Karen Bogenschneider has written more than anyone else in the family studies field about how good research can be used to influence policy decisions, and why that doesn't happen nearly enough. She surveyed researchers who had been involved in carefully planned events with legislators and staff, where their research findings were heard and considered important. Most of the researchers, unfortunately, failed to follow up on these events, leaving the legislators and their staff hungry for a relationship that didn't exist and for additional facts they couldn't obtain.[400] Mental health professionals

---

[400] Friese, B., & Bogenschneider, K. (2009). The voice of experience: How social scientists communicate family research to policymakers. *Family Relations, 58*(2), 229-243.

can have a greater impact on public policy by not just getting involved once, but actively maintaining relationships with policymakers. I'll review her findings more in the next section.

There are many good reasons to be involved in changing policies that don't work well for you, for your profession, or for the clients you serve. While it does happen, most mental health professionals do not get involved in advocacy purely out of self-interest. Instead, we generally respond to our ethical calling to service.

Ethical obligations

The mental health professions have long recognized that with our positions and our expertise comes a responsibility to act not just on behalf of our clients, but also on the larger communities we serve. This means maintaining awareness of the laws and policies that impact our clients, and working to change those policies that are not in the community's best interest as we see it. While our professional organizations may phrase this obligation differently, most of them include it. Organizations' requirements and encouragements for professional advocacy are quoted in the table below. Simply put, you are expected to use your specialized knowledge and training to benefit the larger community. It is part of holding the title of a mental health professional.

Solving real problems

Those mental health professionals who do seek to influence public policy tend not to do it out of a sense of obligation, though. They tend to do this work out of a desire to have an impact on the community that is real, significant, and larger than the impact they can have by working with even a hundred specific cases.

Though their underlying philosophies differ (see "Differences between professions" in Chapter 1), each of the mental health professions seeks to understand the rules that govern human behavior and relationships, and ultimately to have an impact on not just individuals but communities and cultures. It is this notion that tends to draw the therapists most passionate about advocacy work.

Consider, as an example, the statements of various professional organizations on same-sex marriage. While some therapists are understandably reluctant to wade into such a politically controversial area with their professional hat on, mental health researchers have produced a great deal of well-grounded scientific literature on the functioning of families with same-sex couples. We see in our therapy offices the real impacts of discrimination, in the stresses and symptoms of our clients. Who is better equipped than the mental health community to share with legislators the impact of societal oppression on same-sex couples and families, or to inform legislators of what we can safely say we know about the long-term impact of growing up with same-sex parents? If mental health professionals do not fill this information need with good, objective research findings, others will happily fill the information vacuum with pseudoscience or scare tactics. **When mental health professionals inform a debate, it does make a real difference:** When the Iowa Supreme Court ruled that a ban on same-sex marriage was unconstitutional,[401] they heavily cited the policies and findings noted in a brief filed by the American Psychological Association, detailing a number of studies that suggested same-sex couples and their children suffer needlessly from being unable to marry.[402]

This is, of course, simply an example. Your personal politics of course do not need to agree with those of your professional association, and many practitioners oppose same-sex marriage for religious or other reasons. My point here is not to argue with such a viewpoint, but rather to stress the importance of therapists being involved in policy discussions. Even when that means therapists will be representing both sides of a debate, the policymakers involved will be making more fully-informed decisions than they might without the involvement of therapists.

---

[401] The case was formally *Varnum v Brien*. The full ruling of the Iowa Supreme Court can be read here:
hosted.ap.org/specials/interactives/_documents/iowa040309.pdf
[402] The APA brief can be read here:
www.apa.org/about/offices/ogc/amicus/varnum.pdf

Table 10.1: Professional associations' ethical standards supporting advocacy

Association	Code of Ethics Language[403]
AAMFT	**Preamble.** Marriage and family therapists are concerned with developing laws and regulations pertaining to marriage and family therapy that serve the public interest, and with altering such laws and regulations that are not in the public interest.
ACA	**A.7.a. Advocacy.** When appropriate, counselors advocate at individual, group, institutional, and societal levels to address potential barriers and obstacles that inhibit access and/or the growth and development of clients.
AMHCA	**F2. Advocate.** Mental health counselors may serve as advocates at the individual, institutional, and/or societal level in an effort to foster sociopolitical change that meets the needs of the client or the community.
CAMFT	**7.6 Developing Public Policy:** Marriage and family therapists are concerned with developing laws and regulations pertaining to marriage and family therapists that serve the public interest, and with altering such laws and regulations that are not in the public interest.
NASW	**6.04 Social and Political Action.** (a) Social workers should engage in social and political action that seeks to ensure that all people have equal access to the resources, employment, services, and opportunities they require to meet their basic human needs and to develop fully. Social workers should be aware of the impact of the political arena on practice and should advocate for changes in policy and legislation to improve social conditions in order to meet basic human needs and promote social justice.

---

[403] See Appendix for links to each organization's full Codes of Ethics.

▶ Why therapists struggle to influence policy

It seems most therapists are unaware of just how much the BBS
and the state Legislature hunger for their opinions. Therapists
may lack the knowledge of the rulemaking process needed to
advocate well.

Most meetings of the California Board of Behavioral Sciences
(our licensing board) are open to the public. These meetings are the
breeding and testing ground for law and regulation ideas that can
dramatically impact the mental health professions. The 2009 law that
significantly changed the required curriculum in MFT programs, for
example, was developed in a series of open board meetings around the
state where representatives from universities, the profession, and
community agencies all were able to speak about their needs and
desires for changes in MFT degree requirements.

For as important as these meetings are, and as welcoming as
they are to the public, most professionals never go to a BBS meeting.
They wait to be told what happened there by professional associations,
whose representatives are quite often the *only* attendees in the room.

It is ironic, then, that professionals often lament that their
research findings and clinical experience are ignored by policymakers.
Since both policymakers and mental health professionals want the
voice of professionals to be included in policymaking, why doesn't it
happen?

In writing about the difficulty experienced by researchers in
the field of family studies, Bogenschneider developed several
recommendations to promote "a more active, reciprocal engagement"
between policymakers and professionals.[404] Her findings are highly
relevant to the work of mental health clinicians and researchers. She
offers a total of 10 recommendations, paraphrased here:

---

[404] Friese, B., & Bogenschneider, K. (2009). The voice of experience: How
social scientists communicate family research to policymakers. *Family
Relations, 58*(2), 229-243.

1. Think of policy work as developing relationships, not just providing facts
3. Be willing to reach out to policymakers
4. Learn about the policymakers you are working with
5. Communicate information in ways policymakers will understand
6. When discussing vulnerable populations, use clear, specific language
7. Be familiar with the legislative process
8. Provide rapid responses to questions that arise in policy debates
9. Approach policy work as an information provider, not an advocate
10. Respect the wisdom and experience of policymakers
11. Exercise patience and flexibility

A brief comment on her eighth recommendation is important. Bogenschneider was primarily addressing researchers who would be interested in *informing* a policy debate, and not necessarily *taking a position* in that debate. In contrast, this chapter is quite purposefully about taking positions in policy arenas and moving ideas for change forward. However, these are not mutually exclusive. If you are approaching the advocacy process skillfully, you will arrive at policy debates well informed, and your primary investment should be that the problem you have identified gets solved – not a specific *way* that it gets solved. Policymakers and other stakeholders can and will argue about the best methods of solving a problem, and you can provide them with information to move that debate forward. Approach those discussions knowing that everyone involved is doing their best to serve their constituents, and you will be able to engage in a healthy, respectful debate. Even if your efforts are unsuccessful, you will have earned the respect of those on the other side of the issue, which will be helpful when working in the future on the same issue or on any other.

In fact, researchers in Bogenschneider's study pointed to three key rewards of being involved in policy work (paraphrased here), none of which involve being on the winning side of a policy argument:

1. They were able to have a meaningful impact on the community
2. They were able to see their research applied to real-world problems
3. They felt respected for the wisdom and expertise they brought to policy discussions

You can and should experience these same rewards. The policymaking community truly does want to hear from you.

▶ What it takes to be a successful advocate

In a moment, I will discuss the actual process of changing a law, regulation, or policy that you feel is not working for you or your clients. First, it is important to understand the qualities that make for a successful advocate.

Information

Your expertise will be well respected in the policymaking community, particularly when you can make specific recommendations backed up by clearly documented facts. The more you know about the issue at hand, the clearer your arguments will be, and the easier it will be to get stakeholders[405] and policymakers on your side.

Motivation

Passion for change is not a liability in policy work. It is an asset – as long as your passion is harnessed as motivation to inform and to act, rather than to attack. Depending on the issue, it may take months or years to see a change (more on that momentarily), but persistence and a good argument will often win out.

Allies

When you can identify a clear and real problem in policy, you may be surprised at how many existing groups and organizations will take an active interest. The BBS and professional associations are just two examples of groups that have the infrastructure in place to write new rules and lobby legislators; there are also mental health consumer

---

[405] I realize this is the first time I've used this term. In case you aren't familiar with it, in policy circles it tends to be broadly used to categorize all those individuals and organizations who have a "stake" in the outcome of a policy discussion.

groups, family member groups, labor organizations, and special interest groups that, like you, want to get involved when they see that they can have a positive impact.[406] Use what they have to offer! Your passion and information combined with their connections can make for a powerful and effective team.

Patience

Simply put, meaningful change takes time. The fields of family therapy and counseling have been lobbying for Medicare inclusion for almost 10 years now, and continue knocking on the door.[407] The BBS works on a cycle of quarterly meetings, and issues must be put on the agenda for a committee meeting, heard in committee, and forwarded to the full Board before they even vote on it – a process that can easily take six months.

Similarly, the state Legislature operates primarily on an annual cycle. Introducing an issue to a legislator in May might mean that even under the best of circumstances, where the legislator throws their full support behind your proposed solution and is even willing to author a bill that would change the law as you recommended, that bill may not be formally proposed until early the next year. It could be as late as September of the next year before you knew whether your bill made it into law, and that's if your bill wasn't pushed back to the following year.

The time lag can certainly be demotivating at first, but it has a couple of indirect benefits. One is that it allows for careful consideration of the specific language of a proposal, to ensure that it doesn't have unintended consequences. Another is that if you remain heavily involved in pushing your proposal forward, the long process of moving through committee hearings and the rest of the legislative process means that you typically don't need to take huge chunks of

---

[406] For a list of common stakeholder groups in mental health law, see the end of this chapter.

[407] Each profession has gotten a bill through at least one house of Congress, but has not managed to get a Medicare inclusion bill through both houses of Congress at the same time. They are actively working together in Washington on this issue. If you are an MFT or PCC, your national association could use your help!

time out of your job or your private practice to move your idea forward. In theory, that should make it easier for more of us to act on our ideas.

▶ The advocacy process

Now that you know why you should be an advocate, and the qualities you need to have to move a policy idea forward, how do you do it? The process can be broken down into specific stages, each of which I will discuss in some detail:

1. Recognize a problem or concern
2. Identify the specific policy issue
3. Gather information
4. Strategize
5. Take action
6. Adapt and (sometimes) accept compromise
7. Repeat as needed

As you will see, these same steps apply regardless of whether the specific policy concern is institutional (like a concern about a policy at your university), professional (such as a problem with the wording of one of your ethical requirements), legal (something that requires a new law in order to fix), or regulatory (something that requires licensing board action to change a regulation, but does not need the involvement of the legislature).

1. Recognize a problem or concern

Many of us first get into policy work because we can see something that is not working. Maybe a law is having unintended consequences, or the field has changed such that a new policy is needed. When a problem directly impacts you, that can be a powerful motivator to fix the problem – not just for you, but for anyone who may follow you and run into the same problem.

It is helpful at this very early stage to give serious thought to whether your problem is specific to your own immediate situation, or whether it is actually an issue that is likely to impact many others. If the problem only impacts you, you may want to first see whether an exception can be made for your situation before embarking on a much larger process of policy change. For example, if your university has a policy that is negatively impacting you because of unique personal circumstances, you may have the best success by reaching out to your faculty or dean to see what options exist for granting policy exceptions.

2. Identify the specific policy issue

The next step is to very specifically locate the problem. You may know that there is a policy issue, but what is the particular rule that is causing or worsening the problem you see? The BBS publishes an updated booklet each year of the laws and regulations for LMFTs, LPCCs, and LCSWs,[408] which is a good place to start if your problem is in law or regulation. You should find, at this stage, the specific section of law, ethics code, or institutional policy that you want to change.

Naturally, laws and regulations are written in legal language, so you may want or need some help deciphering them. If you are experiencing a problem you believe might be a policy issue, you can work with colleagues, supervisors, or your professional association to find the exact language that is of concern. They also can let you know whether your issue is impacting more of their members.

You may already have a potential solution in mind at this point, but it will be important to not be too locked into that solution at this time. As you will see in the next stages, there may be other solutions available.

3. Gather information

Has anyone else run into the same problem you are now facing? Internet searches, conversations with colleagues, and discussions with your professional association can help answer that question. If others have run into the same issue, how have they gone about trying to resolve it? What solutions were attempted, even if they failed? What were the impacts of those efforts? All of this information will be helpful to you in figuring out how to move forward.

Gathering information also means contacting those groups you believe will be stakeholders in the issue, including (perhaps *especially*)

---

[408] Board of Behavioral Sciences (2014). *Statutes and Regulations Relating to the Practice of Professional Clinical Counseling, Marriage and Family Therapy, Educational Psychology, and Clinical Social Work.* Sacramento, CA: BBS.

those who you believe are likely to disagree with you on the problem or proposed solution. You will not be giving anything away by letting them know you are acting on the issue; they will have plenty of time to hear your concerns and proposed solution no matter what, and coming to them early in the process may lead them to try working with you on a compromise rather than battling against you later.

With all stakeholder groups, you should ask them about their knowledge and experience of the problem, their investment in fixing it (including any previous efforts they may have made), and whether they are interested in working with you in the advocacy process. A good information-gathering process will result in a team of allies, all sharing information, and committed to working together to solve the problem you helped bring to their attention.

4. Strategize

At this stage, if you have stakeholders working with you, you will transition from being an individual with a problem to being part of a team pushing for a specific solution. An adage often repeated by the former Dean at the university where I teach was "Don't bring me problems, bring me solutions." This is a common desire among policymakers. With your team, you will likely discuss and debate several possible avenues for solving the problem, settling on the one that the team believes is most likely to be adopted. You then will work on how to push that idea forward – who needs to talk to whom, when the contacts should be made, and what they hope to get from each stage of the process.

There are two important things to keep in mind at this stage. One is to be a team player. Working as part of a group means accepting the group's wisdom and influence. Stakeholders may have knowledge of the policymaking process that you lack. There is a good balance to be struck between maintaining your personal voice in the process and working with the group to get the problem solved.

The second important thing to keep in mind at this stage is that you are likely to encounter opposition as you push your cause forward. Part of strategizing is anticipating the arguments of those who disagree with you, and being prepared with more convincing responses. With a plan in hand, you can walk into any debate about the issue confident that you have the right plan.

5. Take action

You and your allies have a plan. Now you need to carry it out. Depending on the issue, this can involve meeting with policymakers, letter-writing, phone calls, organizing others with the same concern, involving the media, or any number of additional actions. If the strategy you developed in the previous stage is solid, you simply need to see it through.

If you are part of a group, and the group agreed on a strategy at the previous stage, follow that plan. Make sure you have the understanding and agreement of the group before making any changes to the plan. Venturing away from the agreed-upon plan, even if your intentions are good, risks undermining the group's efforts and ultimately making success less likely. More than once, a coalition with a good plan to change a policy has come unraveled when one member of the group decided to go their own way.

As you are acting toward the change you desired, you will likely find yourself faced with stakeholders who disagree with you. While you may be able to make more convincing arguments and get policymakers to take your side, a better path is to work with those opposing stakeholders and see whether you can come to a point of agreement. If you can address their concerns, you may actually be able to get those stakeholders who initially opposed you to instead help you move the idea forward.

6. Adapt and (sometimes) accept compromise

Even with a good plan there are roadblocks along the way that were not anticipated. Action plans need to be able to adapt to changing circumstances; arguments need to be formulated on the fly when others disagree with you for reasons you had not expected. Adapting your plan and your arguments is a normal part of the process. Particularly in longer change processes such as the process required to get a bill through the legislature, your proposal is likely to be amended along the way.

As the old saying goes, you should not let the perfect be the enemy of the good; a policy change that is a step in the right direction, even if not as big of a step as you were hoping for, is still a success. As mentioned in the previous stage, if your proposal encounters

---

opposition from other stakeholders along the way, see whether your proposal can be changed to address the opposition's concerns. Often policy opposition does not come from disagreement about the nature of the problem, but instead differences in preferred solutions. Legislators are conflict-averse; they like to see stakeholder groups come together to eliminate opposition to bills. As you might expect, it is much easier for them to vote for a bill when they know that their vote will not be angering groups of their constituents.

Accepting compromise works to everyone's benefit. Your idea moves forward, opponents become friends, and policymakers become much more comfortable with accepting whatever it is you have proposed. While compromise is not always possible, it is worth going to great lengths to pursue.

7. Repeat as needed

If you have moved successfully through the previous stages and seen your idea through to the end of the advocacy process, congratulations! You have very likely made a change that will impact significant numbers of professionals or the clients we serve.

Success in policy work is addictive. It brings you new contacts who are like-minded, colleagues or clients who are grateful for your work, and most importantly, a very real, concrete impact on the community around you. Once you have had that success, you may decide that your policy work is done. But that's unlikely. More likely, you will have encountered other policy problems along the way, or been left less-than-fully-satisfied by whatever compromises were made on the journey toward the policy change you initially proposed.

Whatever your specific outcome, I hope you choose to remain active in policy work. Even if it means we will disagree, you are my colleague, you should have a place at the table in policy discussions, and we can make changes that will improve the quality of life for the clients we serve and the professionals who will follow us.

▶ How new rules are made

The most important thing to know about making or changing the rules for a profession is that the rules are meant to be adaptive. They are set forth in living documents, and while the process for changing them should be cautious and deliberative, rules should be able to adapt to changes in the profession and in the larger social environment.

This section outlines in general terms how the rules governing our profession are changed. The process will often vary depending on the kind of problem being solved and just how major or controversial the proposed change is.

Institutional policymaking

Any non-governmental agency – a hospital, a university, a mental health clinic, even a small private practice – has a set of policies and practices it follows. Generally speaking, the larger the institution, the more of its policies will be in writing to ensure that everyone who works there acts in a responsible manner consistent with those policies.

Of course, every specific institution is different. **However, there are some common processes used by larger institutions in changing their policies**. Most will field a suggestion about a new policy or a change in existing policy within some form of committee, tasked with discussing the potential impact of such a change. Often, the person who suggested the change will be invited to speak at a committee meeting, answer questions from committee members, and offer additional detail about the need for the proposed change. Typically, the committee would then make a recommendation to the individual or group who actually has the power to change the policy. Depending on the organization, there may be a second hearing where that person or group again considers the issue.

Professional rulemaking

When discussing the rules that exist on the professional level, we typically are talking about professional Codes of Ethics. Each major mental health association has its own code (links to which are offered in the "Additional Resources" at the end of this chapter).

Ethics codes are updated every few years, though they may be changed more often if the larger professional context demands it. The NASW Code of Ethics was last updated in 2008, making it the most dated current code among the professions discussed here. The AAMFT updated its Code in 2015, ACA in 2014, CAMFT in 2011, and NASW in 2008. In each instance, meaningful updates were made that reflected changing standards within each profession.

Proposed changes to a code of ethics are typically first raised to the association's staff or Board of Directors, who collect such suggestions when there is not an active revision process underway. Once that process has started, a committee of professionals is assigned to review the code and the suggestions collected from members, and consider those in the context of the current professional environment. The committee then recommends specific language to the association's board. Because a code of ethics is binding upon all members of the association, it is typically put before all of the association's members for additional feedback, a broad vote, or both before taking effect.

The California legislative process

The state of California uses a similar process to the one described in "Institutional policymaking," though it is much more structured.[409] The California legislature consists of two houses, or groups of lawmakers: the Assembly and the Senate. If you are a California resident, you are represented by both a state Assembly member and a state Senator. It is helpful to know who your representatives are, as they are especially receptive to input from the specific people they represent.

---

[409] This is a summary and leaves out some key pieces. The Legislature offers its own more detailed explanation of the California legislative process at www.leginfo.ca.gov/bil2lawx.html

Whoever has an idea for a new or amended law must find an *author* – that is, a legislator (from either house) willing to write the bill and formally propose it. Associations and licensing boards typically will have a much easier time convincing legislators to author bills because they have relationships with the legislators; this is part of why it is a good idea to get stakeholder groups on board with your idea before moving forward.

Once a legislator has proposed a bill, it gets assigned to a policy committee for consideration. These committees consider, in detail, the likely effects of the bill; they also accept public input. When outside organizations say they have taken a position on a bill, that typically means they have informed the author and the legislature of their position, and they may also testify about the bill during committee meetings. Most outside groups take positions on bills while they are still in the policy committee stage, to have the most input on the bill.

Next, the policy committee votes on the bill. If they move it forward, it may go to another committee or to the full house (that is, a bill proposed in the Assembly would go to the full Assembly) for a vote. If it passes there, it follows the same process in the other house, starting with the other house's policy committee.

Bills can be amended at any step of the legislative process, up to the final vote of the second house of the legislature. If the bill was amended while going through the second house, there will be a final vote on the amended version of the bill in both houses. Once the final bill has passed both houses, it cannot be further amended. It moves to the Governor for consideration. The Governor must then sign the bill into law, or veto it. If the Governor takes no action, the bill automatically becomes law. A veto can be overridden with a 2/3 vote of both houses. Most bills signed into law take effect January 1 of the next year.

The California regulatory process

Many of the rules that govern California professions come from regulation, and not legislation. The difference is that regulations are put into place by licensing boards and other governmental agencies and do not need the approval of the Legislature or the Governor. They largely serve to make legislation clearer and more specific, so that agencies like licensing boards can apply the rules equally to all of their licensees. Any time there is a conflict between legislation and regulation, the regulation is ignored and the standard set in legislation applies.

When the BBS wants to change regulation, they first determine through staff input, Board and committee meetings what changes need to be made. These meetings are open to the public, and indeed many of the changes to regulation pursued by the BBS come from suggestions made by ordinary licensees or their professional associations.

Once the BBS has decided on specific language, they vote to send the proposal forward to the Department of Consumer Affairs and the state's Office of Administrative Law.[410] If those groups have no suggested changes, the proposed regulations are posted online for a period of public comment. The BBS is required to respond to *every single comment* made during this time, from any individual or organization. They do not need to agree with the comment, but they must offer a justification for why they are refusing that comment or suggestion. They typically get few such comments.

As one recent example, the BBS has been working to change the process of how it handles complaints against its licensees. This process is set in regulation, not legislation, so it must be changed through regulation.

---

[410] The Office of Administrative Law offers a more detailed explanation of the regulatory process here:
http://www.oal.ca.gov/Regular_Rulemaking_Process.htm

▶ Examples of the advocacy process

So far, I have talked in general terms about the process of advocacy. It can be helpful, of course, to see specific examples – including examples of efforts that *didn't* work, so that you will see that sometimes even good efforts fall short.

Below are four examples of the advocacy process at work: the addition of "couple and family therapy" to the acceptable degree titles for MFT licensure in California, the birth of the LPCC license in the state, a failed attempt to clarify the rules about whether interns can pay their employers for supervision, and California's first-in-the-nation ban on so-called "reparative therapy" for minors.

The "couple and family therapy" degree title

I teach for the Couple and Family Therapy programs at Alliant International University in Los Angeles. Like many programs, we used to call our programs "Marriage and Family Therapy" to be consistent with the title of the license. A few years ago, we noticed a trend around the country of programs changing their program names and degree titles to be more inclusive. LMFTs work with many couples who are not married, of course, including gay and lesbian couples who are often legally barred from marriage.

As a faculty, we voted to change the name of our program in a faculty meeting. That was a relatively easy change to make, and a good example of institutional rule changes being easier and faster than changes in state law. But we also wanted to have a conversation about changing our degree title to match the name of our program. (Once the program name had changed, we were a Couple and Family Therapy program, but we were still issuing degrees in "Marriage and Family Therapy.")

Unfortunately, state law at the time would not allow a degree titled "Couple and Family Therapy" to be eligible for LMFT licensure (step 1 of the process described above is to recognize a problem; this was clearly a problem). We were quickly able to identify the section of law that was problematic (step 2), which was section 4980.36 of the California Business and Professions Code. It required all applicants for MFT licensure or intern registration to

"[...] possess a doctor's or master's degree meeting the requirements of this section in marriage, family, and child counseling, marriage and family therapy, psychology, clinical psychology, counseling psychology, or counseling with an emphasis in either marriage, family, and child counseling or marriage and family therapy [...]"

Without "Couple and Family Therapy" on that list, we could not even have a conversation about changing our degree title. A renamed degree would not have been eligible for licensure.

Our next step was to gather information (step 3). We were able to put together a list of COAMFTE-accredited programs around the country who offered degrees titled "couple and family therapy" – and noticed that these degrees would be eligible for licensure in California, since out-of-state degrees are evaluated based on their content rather than their titles.[411]

We also went about talking to stakeholders, which is a key component of step 3. AAMFT-CA was quickly willing to support an effort to add "couple and family therapy" to the list of acceptable degree titles. We also took the issue to other MFT programs around the state to gather support for the change.

In choosing what action to take (step 4, Strategize), we determined that there was not likely to be significant opposition to our proposal. However, because the problem was one of state law, it had to be changed through the legislative process. We chose to work directly with the BBS in hopes that the item could be added to an "omnibus" bill rather than requiring its own separate legislation.[412]

We began the action process (step 5) with a letter to the BBS Licensing and Examination Committee.[413] The committee took up the issue in their June 2010 meeting, where they voted to recommend that

---

[411] California Business and Professions Code sections 4980.74(b), 4980.78(b)(5), and 4980.90(d)(2)
[412] Omnibus bills are used primarily for technical changes and non-controversial changes to the law. These bills typically generate strong bipartisan support – in part because any item that does generate controversy is quickly removed.
[413] You can see a copy of that letter on page 9 of this PDF: http://www.bbs.ca.gov/pdf/agen_notice/2010/0610_licexam_mtg_material.pdf

the full BBS support the change when they would consider the issue. A month later, the full BBS expressed their support for the change.

Thankfully, we did not need to do any compromising (step 6). Committee and BBS members' questions at those two meetings simply sought to ensure that nothing was being removed from the law; we were only adding an acceptable degree title. No other professional associations objected to the change, and with the BBS's vote of support, BBS staff worked with legislators to include the item in the 2011 omnibus bill of the California Senate's Business Professions, and Economic Development committee. That bill was signed by the Governor in September 2011, and the change went into effect in state law on January 1, 2012.

As you can see from this example, even a small change to the law that has broad support and no opposition can take a long time. But the change is meaningful and important, as now graduate programs across the state can issue degrees in "Couple and Family Therapy" if they choose. If programs around the country begin to further change their degree names (perhaps next will be to "Relational Therapy," to clarify that we do work with individuals, just from a relational context), we can go through the process again as needed (step 7).

The LPCC license

For an example of a much more significant change in the law being successful, one need look no further than the very existence of the Licensed Professional Clinical Counselor license in California.

In the early 2000s, LPCs continued earning licensure across the country, and had achieved licensure in most states – but not California. The problem was clear (step 1): Without licensure, those with LPC training could only work in license-exempt settings. Their other option was to try to qualify for an existing form of licensure (such as LMFT), but this would often mean taking significant additional coursework and training. Furthermore, as was the case for LMFTs at the time, having states without licensure laws hindered LPCs' efforts at inclusion in federal programs like Medicare.[414]

---

[414] You'll notice I'm using the abbreviation LPC here, rather than LPCC. The LPCC in California denotes that it is a *clinical* counseling license; that is, it is

To achieve licensure, counselors would need to add a new profession to state law (this was their specific problem, step 2). They developed a coalition of counselors of various types, who banded together and raised funds for their effort under the name "California Coalition for Counselor Licensure." As they gathered information and began work on their proposal (step 3), they quickly found stakeholders to be unwilling to offer what they had hoped for: A broad-based LPC license in California. The BBS was only willing to support a license specific to mental health. Psychologists, social workers, and family therapists wanted specific restrictions on the counseling scope of practice. Making the counselors' journey even more complicated, these stakeholders sometimes had demands that conflicted with those of other stakeholders. Compromising with one stakeholder group would mean alienating another. The issue of grandparenting was particularly problematic: For those licensed in California as LMFTs, how easy or difficult should it be for them to qualify for a counseling license?

The CCCL's first strategy (step 4) was to go through the legislature's "sunrise" process. This is where a new profession seeks to demonstrate the need for licensure in the state. When they pursued this path in 2006 (step 5), their effort ended without a positive recommendation from the sunrise committee.[415] Wisely, the CCCL adapted (step 6), and sought to push forward in negotiations with stakeholders in spite of the failure of the sunrise process. They worked with CAMFT, a key stakeholder, on compromise language on grandparenting that led CAMFT to remove its opposition to counselor licensure. They worked with the BBS on language that would make their license an "LPCC" license specific to mental health. They worked with the California Psychological Association on compromise language around counselors' ability to use psychological tests. They worked with AAMFT-CA on language limiting LPCCs' ability to assess or treat couples or families without first having training to do so. And they worked with all stakeholder groups on the language of the LPCC scope of practice. While these negotiations took years to reach points of

---

specific to mental health work. Other states use a variety of titles for the profession, but the LPC designation is the most broad for including licensed professionals in counseling across the country.

[415] The Assembly Appropriations Committee's January 18, 2006 analysis of AB894 (2005) describes the outcome of the sunrise process on its final page.

agreement, in 2009 the last key stakeholders removed their opposition. The LPCC licensing bill passed through the legislature and was signed by then-Governor Schwarzenegger. The first LPCC licenses in California were issued through grandparenting in 2011, and through the regular licensure process in 2012. Since the 2009 licensure bill, there have been several other pieces of legislation that have clarified the LPCC profession and its place in the law (step 7). These clarifying bills have largely moved forward with minimal opposition.

Interns paying for supervision

Aaron Feldman was launching a counseling agency in 2009, and knew that many agencies around the state were charging their interns for supervision. He faced a dilemma (step 1) in how he would set his agency up: He didn't want to charge his interns to get their training in his agency, but he also didn't want to build an agency that would have to charge higher client fees than others in the area. As he reviewed the law, he didn't think it was legal for employers to charge their employees for supervision (step 2).

He reached out to CAMFT, AAMFT-CA, and the BBS for information and guidance (step 3). Before he could even strategize about how to solve the problem, it became clear that there were mixed opinions about whether a problem actually existed. CAMFT offered a legal opinion that employers could, in fact, legally charge their employees for supervision as long as it was clear to both parties at the beginning of employment that this was part of the employment agreement. The BBS offered a conflicting legal opinion, arguing that the state labor laws prohibit such an arrangement.[416]

To the best of my knowledge, there have been no test cases on the issue, so there has been no opinion offered by those whose opinions would truly be consequential: a judge or the state labor board. The BBS reached out to the labor board for comment on the issue, but the labor board refused requests to send a representative to a BBS meeting or even offer an opinion in writing.

To date, the issue remains unresolved. However, if you are working as an unpaid intern in a for-profit setting, you should familiarize yourself with the federal rules for internships. If your

---

[416] Minutes of the October 2009 meeting of the BBS, page 11

employer is violating those standards, you may be entitled to back wages for the time that you have worked in that setting.[417]

California's ban on reparative therapy for minors

In 2012, California passed a law that made it unprofessional conduct for any therapist to provide so-called "reparative therapy" to minors. This law, the first of its kind in the country, did not originate from the mental health professions themselves. It came from a state legislator, who used the advocacy process effectively to earn the support of most professional associations and many outside groups. The bill that became law in California has since been used as a model in a number of other states.

State Senator Ted Lieu learned about reparative therapy in the months preceding the 2012 legislative session, and was horrified at what he learned (step 1). Reparative therapy – also sometimes known as conversion therapy, or ex-gay therapy – aims to change a client's sexual orientation, based on the assumption that homosexuality is a pathological condition.[418] There is no objective scientific evidence that the therapy is generally effective at changing the sexual orientation of clients, though there are some anecdotal accounts of it working. Unfortunately, there are also many anecdotal accounts of the therapy doing long-term harm to those who have gone through it.[419] The absence of scientific support coupled with the apparent risk of harm from this form of therapy have led all of the major mental health associations to caution against its use. However, none of these organizations have directly banned the practice.[420]

---

[417] I've written about this issue on my blog: www.psychotherapynotes.com/uncategorized/could-an-unpaid-mft-intern-sue-for-wage-theft-and-win/
[418] Nicolosi, J. (2009). *Shame and attachment loss: The practical work of reparative therapy.* Downers Grove, IL: InterVarsity Press.
[419] APA Task Force on Appropriate Therapeutic Responses to Sexual Orientation (2009). *Report of the task force on appropriate therapeutic responses to sexual orientation.* Washington, DC: American Psychological Association.
[420] For an explanation of why they have not banned reparative therapy by name, watch this video: www.youtube.com/watch?v=Ki-TQvVhpi4 (this specific issue comes up at the 4:11 mark)

He brought representatives of all of California's mental health professions together in his office early in the year to see why the professional groups had not explicitly banned the practice of reparative therapy, and whether they would object to his moving a bill forward that would have that effect (step 2). He wanted to know what the relevant dynamics were among mental health professionals (step 3).

Working with the associations and with other interested groups (step 4), Senator Lieu initially put forward a bill (step 5) that would have allowed therapists to provide reparative therapy for adults if the therapist engaged in a very specific informed consent process with the client, acknowledging that there was little evidence of success and the possibility of significant risk with this form of treatment.[421]

The professional associations all objected to this approach. Advocacy work sometimes means looking out for how rules might be misused and misinterpreted, and this was a great example of such a time. The associations feared that this informed-consent process would actually be creating a "safe haven" for the practice of reparative therapy, putting into law that California found the practice to be within legal requirements (the fact that it included specific conditions for informed consent did not resolve this issue).[422] Far better, the associations felt, to leave the law gray than to have a specific statement in the law that reparative therapy was allowed, even with restrictions.

So Senator Lieu and his staff wisely regrouped, and worked with the associations on a better approach (step 6). When he changed his bill to make it a simple ban on reparative therapy for minors, he quickly earned the support of NASW-CA and AAMFT-CA, and most other professional associations ultimately joined this support.

The bill was signed by the Governor in September 2012, and immediately challenged in court. Supporters of the bill remained engaged in the process, submitting dozens of amicus briefs (these are papers used to inform courts about the underlying scientific or legal

---

[421] Senate Bill 1172 (Lieu), 2012. Use the pull-down menu in the upper right corner to select the April 9, 2012 version.

[422] Caldwell, B. E., & Kahn, A. C. (2012). California prohibits therapists from working to change a minor's sexual orientation. *Family Therapy Magazine*, *11*(6), 8-11. Available online at newsmanager.commpartners.com/aamft/downloads/CaldwellArticle.pdf

issues in a case, filed by individuals or groups who are not directly involved; "amicus" here means "friend of the court") arguing that the law should be allowed to take effect.[423] The fight went all the way to the US Supreme Court; when they refused to hear the case, the law finally did take effect.[424]

This is an example of a very time-consuming, but ultimately effective, advocacy effort. It demonstrated the importance of all of those factors listed earlier in this chapter: Information, motivation, allies, and patience. The change it made in state law was significant, protecting untold numbers of children from the potentially damaging effects of reparative therapy. Had the bill not been signed by the Governor, or had it been defeated in court, its proponents surely would have tried again, using knowledge gained from that failure (step 7). However, in this instance, they didn't need to.

Instead, the California law has been a model for those debated in at least eight other states, including laws passed in New Jersey and the District of Columbia. Now that California's law has survived its court challenge, it seems likely that other states will feel safer in following suit. The initial efforts of just a few advocates in California will thus continue to have impact all around the country.

---

[423] All amicus briefs filed in this case at the US Ninth Circuit Court of Appeals can be found here:
www.ca9.uscourts.gov/content/view.php?pk_id=0000000635
[424] McGreevy, P. (2014 June 30). Supreme Court rejects challenge to law banning gay-conversion therapy. *Los Angeles Times.* Available online at www.latimes.com/local/political/la-me-pc-california-supreme-court-gay-conversion-therapy-20140630-story.html

▶ Be the change

In closing, let me offer perhaps an overly-brief summary of this text: You've learned many of the specific rules governing master's-level mental health professionals in California, and just as importantly, you've learned how to change those rules that aren't working very well.

I hope you will join me and your professional associations in that task of change. As you will see many times through your career as a therapist, sometimes actions taken with the best of intentions have negative consequences. And, as you will also see many times through your career as a therapist, simple insight into these failures is not enough. **We do neither our clients nor our professions any favors if all we ever do about the rules that govern our lives is talk.** When something in life – whether it be the life of a client, or the life of a profession – isn't working, our calling should be develop understanding *and then to act,* thoughtfully and collaboratively, to fix the problem.

One of my greatest joys as a teacher has been seeing my students take up this charge, becoming advocates for their clients and their professions in the truest sense of the word. I hope and trust that you will do the same.

I look forward to working with you.

Appendices

▶ List of Tables

▶ Topic Index

Consultants, 44
Couple and family restriction for
   LPCCs, 34, 158-159
Criminal cases, 86
Criminal convictions, 91
CSWE, 76

D

Danger to others, 139-142
Danger to property, 142-143
Danger to self, 135-138
Degrees (in advertising), 204
Department of Consumer
   Affairs, 108, 171, 250
Dependent adult abuse
   definition of dependent adult,
   178-179
   reasonable suspicion, 183
   reporting, 180-186
Directories, 194
Disciplinary actions, 86
Disciplinary process, 102-107
Driving under the influence
   (DUI), 113
Drug use
   see Impairment
   see Uniform Standards Related
   to Substance Abuse
Duty to protect, 139-141

E

Elder abuse
   definition of elder, 178
   reasonable suspicion, 183
   reporting, 180-186
Electronic health records, 223-
   224
Email, 194, 227

Emotional abuse
   see Child abuse
Ewing v. Goldstein, 141
Exams
   see Licensing exams
Exempt settings, 48

F

Facebook, 94, 123, 196-197
Fees
   advertising, 208
   disclosure, 97, 118
   for referrals, 97
Fictitious business names, 202
5150 holds, 138
Firearms
   see Guns
Flyers, 194
Fraud, 86, 92
Freedom of speech, 84

G

General misconduct, 99-100
Google ads, 198
Gross negligence, 99-100
Guns, 141

H

Health Grades, 155, 208
HIPAA, 119, 143, 219-222
Hospitalization, 137-138, 142

I

Impairment, 90, 108-109
Impersonation, 92
Incompetence, 99-100

Informed consent, 99, 115-129, 218
  with minors, 128-129
  technology-based services, 99, 119, 218
Internet advertising
  see Advertising
Internet therapy
  see Technology
Interns, 39
  advertising, 192, 209-212
  MFT, 53, 210
  PCC, 77, 212
Investigations, 104-105

L

License exemptions, 47-48
License renewals, 47
License requirements, 45-82
Licensing exams
  process, 61-62, 74-75, 80-81
  restructure, 63, 75, 82
  security, 93-94
Life coaches
  see Coaching

M

Misconduct
  see Unprofessional conduct

N

NAMI California, 268
NASW, 269
NASW-CA, 268
NCMHCE, 74-75
Negligence, 99-100
Networking groups, 213-214

No harm contracts, 136
Notice of Privacy Practices, 119

O

Ombudspersons, 184
Online therapy
  see Technology

P

Policymaking, 232-238, 247-250
Privilege, 133, 146-149
Practicum, 39, 52-54, 66-68
Probation
  see Disciplinary actions
Professional Therapy Never Includes Sex, 89
Professional titles, 199-203
Progress notes, 150-151
Professional liability insurance, 111
Psychological testing, 31, 34
Psychologists, 25
"Psychotherapy" and "psychotherapist" in advertising, 202-203

R

Recklessness, 99-101
Records
  disposal, 152-153
  maintaining, 97, 152
  requests for records, 151-152
  storage, 152-153
  see also Progress notes
Registrant
  definition, 19
Regulations, 249-250

▶ Directory of key stakeholder groups

The following groups can be useful allies on issues where state policy would benefit from a change. They are organized here into three categories: Government; Consumer, Family, and Provider Organizations; and Professional Organizations. If you have suggestions for organizations to add to this list for future editions, please feel free to send them! See "About the Author" on page 271.

Government

Board of Behavioral Sciences
1625 North Market Blvd., Suite S-200
Sacramento, CA 95834
www.bbs.ca.gov

Board of Psychology
1625 North Market Blvd., Suite N-215
Sacramento, CA 95834
www.psychboard.ca.gov

Department of Consumer Affairs
Consumer Information Division
1625 North Market Blvd., Suite N-112
Sacramento, CA 95834
www.dca.ca.gov

Department of Health Care Services
(mailing address varies by program)
www.dhcs.ca.gov

Consumer, Family, and Provider Organizations

California Council of Community Mental Health Agencies
1127 11th St., Suite 925
Sacramento, CA 95814
www.cccmha.org

National Alliance on Mental Illness, California
1851 Heritage Ln., Suite 150
Sacramento, CA 95815
www.namicalifornia.org

State Professional Organizations

**American Association for Marriage and Family Therapy,
California Division**
PO Box 6907
Santa Barbara, CA 93160
www.aamftca.org

**California Association for Licensed Professional Clinical
Counselors**
1240 India Street, Unit 1302
San Diego, CA 92101
www.calpcc.org

California Association of Marriage and Family Therapists
7901 Raytheon Rd.
San Diego, CA 92111
www.camft.org
CAMFT Code of Ethics
www.camft.org/Content/NavigationMenu/AboutCAMFT/
CodeofEthics/default.htm

**National Association of Social Workers,
California Chapter**
1016 23rd St.
Sacramento, CA 95816
www.naswca.org

National Professional Associations

American Association for Marriage and Family Therapy
www.aamft.org
AAMFT Code of Ethics:
www.aamft.org/imis15/content/legal_ethics/
code_of_ethics.aspx

American Counseling Association
www.counseling.org
ACA Code of Ethics:
www.counseling.org/Resources/aca-code-of-ethics.pdf

American Mental Health Counselors Association
www.amhca.org
AMHCA Code of Ethics:
http://www.amhca.org/about/codetoc.aspx

National Association of Social Workers
www.socialworkers.org
NASW Code of Ethics:
www.socialworkers.org/pubs/code/code.asp

▶ Additional resources

Licensing

California Board of Behavioral Sciences
www.bbs.ca.gov

California Law

Full text of the California Business and Professions Code
leginfo.legislature.ca.gov/faces/codes.xhtml (choose BPC)

Statutes and Regulations for BBS-governed mental health professionals
www.bbs.ca.gov/pdf/publications/lawsregs.pdf

▸ About the author

Benjamin E. Caldwell, PsyD, is a practicing Marriage and Family Therapist (California license number MFC42723) who regularly teaches Law and Ethics classes for Alliant International University in Los Angeles. He has served as chair of the Legislative and Advocacy Committee for the California Division of the American Association for Marriage and Family Therapy, and was honored for his service in 2013 with the AAMFT Division Contribution Award. His research has been published in the *Journal of Marriage and Family Therapy, American Journal of Family Therapy, Journal of Couple and Relationship Therapy*, and in *Family Therapy* and *Self* magazines. He maintains a private practice specializing in the treatment of distressed couples. He lives in Los Angeles, CA.

(Photo by Tracy Teague / Trace Images, courtesy Casey Caldwell.)

Other books by Ben Caldwell

Becoming a Marriage and Family Therapist: 24 essays
California Family Therapy Program Rankings: 34 of the state's best MFT programs

Find me online

My web site: www.BenCaldwell.com
My Facebook page: www.facebook.com/bencaldwellpsyd
My Twitter feed: www.twitter.com/bcmft
My blog on policy, research, and professional issues in marriage and family therapy: www.PsychotherapyNotes.com

▶ Questions, comments, or corrections

This book has a web site all its own, where you can see reviews (and submit yours), submit suggestions and corrections, join my email list (I don't share your information with third parties), and see how new editions are coming along. The site is www.CALawBook.com. You are also welcome to email me directly at ben@bencaldwell.com.

As mentioned at the opening to this text, I am not an attorney, so I regret that I cannot offer advice for particular situations. For such questions, please consult with a qualified legal professional. But for everything else, I would love to hear from you!